10 THINGS AMERICANS
WISH THEY HAD KNOWN

AND 7 THINGS
THEY HAVE TO KNOW

Amazing and Accurate Prophecies About What the Future Holds

BISHOP E. BERNARD JORDAN

FOGHORN
PUBLISHERS
"Of Making Many Books There Is No End..."

Ten Things Americans Wished They Had Known And Seven Things They Have to Know

All Scripture quotations, unless otherwise indicated, are taken from the Holy Bible, New International Version® NIV® Copyright 1973, 1978, 1984 by International Bible Society, The King James Version, and the Amplified Version. Used by permission.

Zoe Ministries
310 Riverside Drive
New York, NY 10025
212-316-2177
212-316-5769 fax

ISBN-10: 1-934466-22-0
ISBN-13: 978-1-934466-22-3
Printed in the United States of America
©2009 by E. Bernard Jordan. All Rights Reserved.

Foghorn Publishers
P.O. Box 8286
Manchester, CT 06040-0286
860-216-5622
www.foghornpublisher.com
foghornpublisher@aol.com

PROPHETIC PARTNERS

Prophetess Rosonya Adil

Prophetess Nichelle Austin

Ladonna Austin

Prophet Dele Awomolo

Pamela Ball

Prophetess Gina Barber

Opal Barnes

Prophetess Yasmin Best

Yamar Blackburn

Prophetess Elizabeth Bobbitt

Patricia Boone

Tammy Bostick

Prophet Steven &
   Prophetess Veronica Bostick

Prophetess Gloria Boyce

Prophet Ralph Boyce

Tyrone Brackens

Prophet Henry &
   Prophetess Donna Browne

Prophetess Paulette Butler

Charisma Carter

Prophetess Cynthia Clark

Chandra Clement

Prophetess Velma Cody

Prophetess Mascareen Cohen

Tobica Cohen-Williams

Mike Colbert

Prophetess Marchell Coleman

Prophet Harris & Vicki Crooks

Prophetess Jane Danielsen

Prophet Winston &
   Prophetess Evelyn Davis

Cynthia Davis

Prophetess Melody Dickey

Prophetess Deborah Donohue

Susie Enoch

Prophetess Theresa Evans

Prophetess Tangela Flemming

Prophet Billy Gaines

Margaret Grant

Prophet Fitzroy Green

Prophetess Paula Greene

Prophet Mark &
Prophetess Suzette Guy

Prophetess Lisa Harrigan

Michelle Harris

Prophetess Antoinette Harris

Candida Hinton

Marquan Hood-Davis

Malcolm Howard

Redell Hubbard

Maurice Hudson

Prophetess Alice Jackson

Prophetess Umeki Jackson

Prophetess Cleola Johnson Williams

Prophetess Debra Jordan

Prophet Yakim Jordan

Prophetess Mary Jordan

Prophet Donald &
Prophetess Gloria Kelley

Prophetess Bernadine Kelley

Cheryl Kemp

Yaroslav Kirillov

Prophetess Annie Lang

Prophetess Lorna Larmond

Verleiz Latimore

Alvin Lattimore

Audrey Lawrence

Rose LeClaire

Prophet Marcus Legall

Judith Lewin

Prophet Jean Loiseau

Rev. Bessie Mahone

Lorraine Mathis

Prophet Samuel Mays

Prophetess Veronica McKune

Jacquelyn Millette

Glanville Mitchell

Chawnetta Moore

Prophetess Kaneen Morgan

Prophetess Maryann O'Connell

Destiny Ollie

Tanjila Palmer

Prophetess Pearl Parmley

Prophet Darryl Peace

Daniel Peamon

Prophet Omar Plummer

Prophetess Wendy Pompey

Prophet Jason Porter

Prophet Anthony Reid

Tracy Reid

Prophetess Melanie Richards

June Robinson

Prophetess Yolanda Rojas

Prophet Michael &
Prophetess Lynetta Ruble

Prophetess Terry Samuels

Anthony Sanders

Prophetess Pamela Sherrod

Walter &

  Prophetess Joycelyn Shinn

Linda Snyder

Lakeeta Spencer

Prophetess Michelle Starr

Frankie Stockton, Jr.

Karen Stokes

Prophetess Daiya Sykes

Lisa Taylor

Prophetess Patricia Taylor

Prophetess Gloria Thomas

S. Cheryl Thomas

Jerrad Thomas

Prophet Devon Thompson

Governor Cedric &

  Prophetess Dawne Thompson

Prophetess Sonia Tracey

Catherine Turner

Prophet Ivory Underhill

Bertha Ward

Mabel Wariso

Prophetess Joyce Watkins

Leotorah Watson

Prophetess Evelyn Whitfield

Evelyn Williams

Prophetess Linda Williams

Prophetess Sharon Williams

Michelle Winston

April Witherspoon

FOREWORD

"Oh! He that hath eyes, let him see! He that hath feet, let him run this race with diligence! He that hath ears, let him hear what the Spirit is saying! And he that hath a mouth, let him speak that which I am saying, for I shall speak here, there, and everywhere! The earth shall be filled with My Word and with demonstration of My power." As the Word of the Lord was declared in my ears, I beheld that which was strange, yet familiar to my eyes. Then the question did come forth, "Who will go up and who will speak forth My decree in this earth? For I will judge," saith the Lord of Hosts, "and My judgments are righteous. I am the judge of the universe. Do not limit Me, nor question My doings. I shall always do that which pleases Me. I call My people to attention, that they may hear, know and understand that I am the One that has the last word, not you, nor the devil. My Word is the final standard of judgment.

Satan has released many diabolical things in My earth which is Mine and the fullness thereof. He has tried to make My people believe the lie instead of the truth, for My Word is truth. The lie is the image that the world paints before your eyes. Now is the time that My Spirit and My Word shall unite, for they are one and they will agree. The birthing forth of My glorious Church shall come forth and nothing by any chance shall stop it from coming forth in this day and in this generation. I do open up the heavens once again, and to them that will look up and see Me, strength and revelation shall be their portion. But unto them that will not look up to Me as their Source of Life, death shall be their ingestion.

Ask of Me, and I shall remove the scabs from your eyes and anoint you with My heavenly eye salve so that you will clearly understand My doings. Choose even now, saith the Lord. "Choose life! Glory not in your own strength and in the strength of others. But glory in Me, for I reign in glory and majesty! I have reserved a remnant that will move fully into My purposes. I am calling My remnant forth so that they may be trendsetters and partakers of My grace and power. Fear not, for those that are appointed to fulfill My purposes must eat the whole roll, and it shall be sweet unto many and bitter unto others. Do not say in your heart, 'Why must I eat this roll?' For it shall be with obedience and love that I shall show you the way.

Heed My callings! For these are good days for many! These are the days of My wondrous visitation, and many will see it as glorious, and others will see it as damnable. I am calling My people into battle, not a sabbatical. The call has gone out! Arm yourself! Get on course! Many are walking in a wrong course! Get on course, for My people are to walk hand in hand together, conquering the enemy and forever being victorious! I do summon those that are on the Lord's side! I will expose everything that has been hidden and cause it to come to the light! Now is the time of the revealings of your God. Prepare yourself! Prepare yourself! Prepare yourself!

Submitted by His Handmaiden,
Prophetess Debra Jordan

TABLE OF CONTENTS

INTRODUCTION

These are the days the Lord is bringing forth truth and revelation to the Body of Christ in the earth. You will find in this book things that the Father will speak to our generation and generations to come. In light of the revelation, you will hear the Word of the Lord that will sound as a clear trumpet in the earth. The problem will not be in hearing the trumpet, but in having the ability to hear a distinct sound and to interpret the Father's purpose in this hour to affect generations to come.

In reading this book you must have what the Scripture says in Proverbs 20:12, "The hearing ear, and the seeing eye, the Lord hath made even both of them." If you will allow the Holy Spirit to open up your spiritual ears and eyes, you will find your part in the purposes of God for your generation and you will experience a sense of destiny as you allow the Word of the Lord to unfold in these pages.

As the Holy Spirit brings truth and illumination, often individuals become shaken because of the brightness of the light. This book is a continuation of *Written Judgments Part 1,* and in it you will find that the Holy Spirit is speaking to this age and the ages to come. It will be a time of making adjustments to the light that the Holy Spirit will bring forth in this hour.

There is a Divine Verdict in the mouth of our King, and He will cause a generation to emerge with answers and solutions that will cause the powers that be to come into focus on another level which the earth has never seen.

Part I

1

"These are the days," saith the Lord, "that I am raising up major voices in the earth. You will hear voices that you have never heard before. These are the days when I will cause My People to hear sounds in the earth that will terrify some because the sound will not be familiar voices they once knew. It will be a time when you will see new governments come into the place and the world systems will become more and more visible. It will be the time when men will eradicate former laws and set new laws into motion. You will begin to hear major distinct voices, and I will cause a people to emerge in the earth that will take forth My Word unto generations they have never known," saith the Lord.

"This is the time that you will see the changing of the guard taking place within the strata of world leaders, and I will cause nations that have been oppressed to become nations of power in generations to come.

"You will see that the day of the captive prisoners shall be over," saith the Lord, "for it is the hour of the unveiling of My purpose."

Prepare!!... For the new sounds in the earth will be the voices of immorality and you will see and hear things that will not be explainable to a generation that once was. It will be a time of trouble as you have never seen. In this hour you will hear the voices of church leaders emerge, but in this time their persecution will be greater than the earth has ever known. It will be the hour that the world will look for a people to blame for the mass confusion of their day. They will look and find a people that has carried My Name and the world shall hate them for the world's sake," saith the Lord.

In your days, you will see voices writing you from the prisons. The church will continue but a new force will begin to well up in My people and it will be the power of My Spirit," saith the Lord. "I will bring you to a place of understanding the armor of the Lord, and you will find that rest and safety will only be found in Me," saith the Lord. "It will be the day of great awakening, and you will find that a people will emerge from within a people, and you will see the coming forth of the fire of the Lord. In this hour, you will hear the miraculous and prophetic voices that will sound out against demonic voices. It will be a time that you will not have any problem determining which voices are prophetic and which voices are demonic.

There is the coming forth of a people in this time that will bring forth the fire and judgments of the Lord. It will be the season of signs and wonders in the earth as the church and the world has never known. Be prepared for the revolution that is coming in the earth," saith the Lord.

"In this hour I will cause you to hear the seed that has come through great persecution, and you will hear their voices, and they will be the 'Moses' of their day," saith the Lord. "It will be during this time, that a people which I have brought into the earth for reasons that are unknown, will have come forth out of the womb. You will see the coming forth of a generation that will open up the 21st century with trumpets and bring great conflict to the leaders in the earth. I will cause them to appear unto the Pharaohs of their day, and they will speak the judgment of the Lord unto an apostate system; it will be the system of the beast. Prepare yourselves, oh people of the Lord, for the voices in the earth will be voices that are not familiar to thine ears! I will cause your sons and daughters in the 21st century to send forth shock waves that the earth has never felt," saith the Lord. "It will be the days of the emerging of My people in degrees that the earth has never known.

You will see the generation of mockery arise in the manner that the earth has never seen. It will be the time where men will laugh at those who have standards," saith the Lord. "But I will turn the mockery and you will hear a shout of laughter and triumph come out of the camp of My servants," saith the Lord. "It will also be the time that the church structures will take on new dimensions, and you will see a people moving with a new degree of glory upon them. Prepare your hearts for things that you have never seen or heard before."

Then I begin to hear the Lord say, "Come up to a place where I can show you prayers that have been uttered, and I will cause you to understand that you will see greater degrees of unity in the earth such as you've never seen before. It will be the day that I will cause you to understand that there will be no infraction within My Body," saith the Lord. "I will cause the places that have brought a spirit of isolation within My people to be driven out by My Spirit," saith the Lord. "You will see the hour of the unveiling of deceptive spirits and operation of satanic forces and I will bring forth their exposure by My Body coming into perfection in degrees that the Church has never known before," saith the Lord.

"The hour of transition is coming to the people of the Lord. It will be a time of visitation but in these days of visitation you will see the dwelling of the Lord in your midst. I will cause a people to emerge that will understand the value of relationship.

"You will hear the voice of the young cry out for an inheritance that they will not be able to handle. They will waste it in the places of the systems of the world. I will cause My people to accentuate the voices of the young and the old, for it will not be one that is distinguishable by age but by the degree of My wisdom that dwells within them," saith the Lord. "It will be the time of a young and vibrant generation that will come forth on the heels of generals that are in the forefront, but many will push for a premature voice in the earth. These will be the voices of the prodigal sons crying out in the earth. They will be major voices in their day," saith the Lord. "I will bring forth clarity, and you will see the young and the old reconciled in this hour, for it will be the time of the coming together of all the parts of My Church," saith the Lord.

he Word of the Lord came unto my saying, "Now is the time to speak unto the nations that sit in the Middle East. It will be the day of great fury and upset. I will cause the seed of Abraham that has come from the bondwoman to expand at a greater capacity than the earth has ever seen. It will be the day when they will come into power at a very high level.

It will be the day that you will see the religious kingdoms emerge to great heights and power. You will hear of their influence in nations that have borne the Name of My Son, Jesus. It will be the day that you will see them come to power on all levels, but I will cause the seed of the free woman to bring forth things that have never been known or even imagined. It will be the day that the Gospel of the Kingdom will bring change, for I will raise up those that will have the spirit of Caleb and Joshua to bring the word of the Lord unto them without fear or comprise. They will bring them into the reality of My Son, Jesus."

It will be the day that the world of free enterprise will take off in mammoth ways. Nations that you never thought would come into the forefront shall lead in some of the greatest economic developments that the earth has never known.

It will be the time that the faces shall change on your currency," saith the Lord, "and man shall have the audacity to remove Me off their currency. When you see this, I will bring your economy to shame because they will have failed to lift up My Name. It will be the day of changing tides. You will see a nation emerge that will hold strong to value systems, but My Name will not be in their mouths. I will cause a strong undercurrent to come forth in the earth that will declare My plans and My will in degrees that will bring forth revival. You will see the handwriting on the wall and the nations that have experienced My glory in the past shall see 'Ichabod' written on their gate," saith the Lord.

"It will be the time that the seed of the bondwoman will lead in one of the greatest wars in the history of the earth. It will be the day where peace and safety will be scarce in the earth for those that dwell not in the Kingdom of God. I will raise up places of habitation that will be spared from this wrath, but it will only be those places that have recognized My Presence," saith the Lord.

"In this hour, the voices of prophets that will speak of My Kingdom will emerge from obscurity. You will see the Word of the Lord coming forth with great power. Signs and wonders that will be awesome to the natural mind will appear in ways that the earth has never seen to cause people to know that of a truth, I, the Lord, hath spoken."

Then I began to look up into the heavens and I saw a crow coming to the earth. I asked the Lord, "What is the meaning of the crow that descends upon the earth?" And He said unto me, "It is the day that I shall raise up a people that will not become afraid of images that have emerged in the earth to frighten them off. You will see that things which have appeared so powerful are as vapor in My sight."

Then I looked up and said "Lord, what is this sign that is appearing in the heavens?" I saw a great people but their faces were in shrouds. I asked, "Who are they?" He said, "That will be the question that shall circulate around the earth. I will cause them who have known My Name to meet them face to face. It will be the time in the earth that they will bring war, but you will not be able to distinguish their features," saith the Lord. "It will be the time of great development, and

you will see war on the earth that will be fought at an extremely high level of technology.

In this season you will see the eagle, however, the eagle will take its flight. Many will say, 'Where has the eagle gone?'

It will be the day that the lion, the bear, and the eagle will join together in ranks to put an end to the people that are distinguishable.

It will be the day of major upheavals, and you will see My Hand working in ways that the minds of men will not be able to fathom," saith the Lord.

"Come now, and allow Me to show you the works of My Hand, and you will see that I am a God who sets up nations and takes them down," saith the Lord. "It will be the day of weeping for some and joy for others.

When your eyes behold the hour of extreme climate changes in the earth, recognize that a day is coming forth of new frontiers. This will be the day of the coming forth of the oppressed. I will do a new thing in the earth, and you will hear of nations that will carry the gospel at an accelerated pace. Many will come to the knowledge of Me in a major season of harvest," saith the Lord.

"This is now the time when I will cause the nation that holds the hammer and the sickle to come into the forefront for one of the greatest revivals of its day," saith the Lord. "It will be a time of tremendous harvest. You will see the church emerge once again in heights that the earth has never known. It will be the hour that the youth of that land will come forth with sickles to glean the fields for harvest. Teams of evangelism shall come out that land," saith the Lord. "The wind of reversal shall blow, and your eyes shall gaze with astonishment, for the church will be free in the land of the sickle and bound in the land of the eagle.

These will be days that I will cause the oppressed to come forth," saith the Lord. "It will be the time of the coming forth of those that have been concealed by the shadow of My Hand."

Mine eyes beheld the kangaroo as it burst out of obscurity. I asked, "Lord, what is this that is springing forth in the earth?" He replied, "A people who have received a measure of My Word will now begin to see others who have been in bondage come forth to claim that which has been robbed from them," saith the Lord.

> *"It will be the day that the kangaroo's pouch will be filled with great tension, for that which has been hid within the darkness of the pouch is going to come to light in the century to come. I will cause foreigners to enter upon the shores. Oh! So great is the tension that will be felt in that land!*

I will call thee to prayer," saith the Lord, "and you will see Me move in your midst. During those days, the church shall cry out in prayer, but the time will come that I will cause the places that have not seen a demonstration of My Spirit to come into a season of great renewal," saith the Lord. "You will see the purposes of the Lord revealed in degrees that the earth could never conceive. These will be the days that I will cause a firm and mature growth to come within My people in this hour," saith the Lord.

My eyes began to wander, and I focused upon Capitol Hill. I saw things were incomprehensible to the natural mind. I questioned the Lord concerning the things that I saw, and He said, "These are the days that I will bring to light all the hidden works of darkness. Come! Behold My doings in this hour! I will cause a move of My Spirit to enter into this nation, and you will find men that have rejected My Spirit bowing their knees to the majesty of My Name. This will be the time that you will find men who shall enter by the way of the back door, and they shall undergird this nation in prayer. You will see the prophets going in with the Word of the Lord. You will see the young being called to serve in the armed forces and a deficiency of bread across the land, and this shall be the sign that shall proclaim the dawning of this day. It will be the day that the price of wheat will reach an all time high and farmers will be on the upswing in this nation once again," saith the Lord.

I looked up and saw major planets colliding.

I said, "What is the meaning of this?" The Lord said, "It is a day that does await the earth in the pathways of her destiny. You will hear of things seen and unveiled in your galaxy that will be unheard of," saith the Lord. "I will cause things to come within your universe that will be astounding to the minds of natural men. You will see a resurgence of the occult and there will be much spiritual activity taking place within the earth in those days," saith the Lord.

I looked up and then I saw a strange creature that had the face of an owl on the body of a bear and a dragon. The Lord said, "It will be during this time that certain nations will take the eagle in its own craftiness, and you will see the dealings of the Lord made manifest in that land. These are the days when a generation will come into focus that will wage war with these beasts but their tactics will be so unfamiliar, you will find many that will come under their spell," saith the Lord. "I will cause this beast to use a system that has worked for the eagle and it shall begin to soar in great loftiness," saith the Lord. "I will rush you towards this day very shortly, and you will see the purpose of the Lord in degrees that you have never known."

Then I looked up far into the heavens and I saw a man holding an hourglass within his hand. The sand in the hourglass was whiter than white. I saw a blackbird flying around the head of the man. The sand was just about to run out, and I heard a call for the fowl of the air to prepare for its journey to the earth. I heard screams coming out of the nations that had confederated together, and I said, "Lord, what are they crying over?" He said, "The time is not yet for this to be revealed, but I will cause you to see the day of great gathering. The seeds that come after you will see the day of a civil war. History shall repeat herself in a major way, and this shall open in the middle of a century," saith the Lord.

"I will cause you to see a day of great revival come to the lands that have held up its destiny. As England and Germany experience their day of visitation, their economy shall become strong. You will know that revival is about to take place in those lands," saith the Lord.

"You will see My Hand visit the earth in a generation that has raised its hand against Me and My Christ, and I will bring to silence the voices of anti-Christ, and you will hear the laughter of the Lord. Oh! Rejoice, My children! For it is not the day of mourning for thee, but a day of laughter!

The coming judgment in the earth are for redemptive purposes," saith the Lord. "This is now the time that you will see a change in church structure coming forth in the 21st century. A new country and a new people shall come forth in the earth. It will be the time that you will hear of much weeping, but a people that are oppressed will be lifted out of their oppression.

"I call to record young and old to seek My Face, for in the hour of trial there will be a call to choose between Me and the world systems. It is a day that they will desire to turn your places of worship into museums, and they will blame the religious systems for the turmoil of the nations, but be not alarmed," saith the Lord. "I will pour out My wrath upon the children of darkness.

It will be a season of great darkness such as the earth has never seen. It will be as though all time was suspended. During this period, nothing pertaining to the knowledge of man will move forward. For since the light of my Church has grown dim, so will the light of mankind become dim in the areas of music, culture, art, dance, science and medical research. Gross diseases shall multiply, and out of this age will I bring forth a greater people than that which your eyes have ever seen. I will cause the elimination of entire government systems and much of what you look at as history will be lost during this period of time," saith the Lord.

"Out of this period will arise a people stronger than the earth has ever known. It will be a people whose mind will cause them to excel faster than any generation that has ever dwelt upon the earth. Oh! I will cause the heavens to rejoice in this season! It will be the day that technology will cause My purpose to unfold—not only around this planet, but the universe will behold My coming and doings," saith the Lord.

"The people called 'the watchful eye' shall emerge into view. I have called into place ages that have not yet been seen to come into focus for generations that are yet to be born. It will become important for those who know My Name to cause the seed of My Word to be found in the seeds that are to be born in the century to come," saith the Lord.

"I will cause another age to come into place that will cause mankind to see Me in ways that they have never known Me," saith the Lord. "It will be the time of the space age. I will cause communication from the heavenly realm to be piped into the ears of the earth," saith the Lord. "You will hear the music of the universe that will be discovered, and you will hear the stars singing through technology that is yet to be born in the earth.

I will cause instruments to come into the earth that she is not familiar with," saith the Lord. "It will be a day that you will see the unveiling of My purpose that has been hidden for generations.

It will be the time that inventions shall come forth at an accelerated pace. It will be known as the day of witty inventions.

Come away, My beloved, and allow Me to show you things that will cause you see another side of My purpose," saith the Lord. "You are coming into a time where you will find that the world is too small," saith the Lord. "Not small in terms of land mass, but small in terms of the levels of communication and transportation that will expand at phe"Come now and allow Me to show you that the heavens declare My glory. It will be a season of the coming of My Presence in the earth in degrees that will baffle the minds of men. For many are looking for Me in places that they will not find Me moving in this hour. I will be appearing in unexpected places, and religious people will have a hard time as they try to comprehend what I am doing," saith the Lord.

3

Fathers

"This will be the time that I will bring a reformation of leadership within My Church," saith the Lord. "It will be the day of the fathers that will be seen in the earth. In this season, you will find those that I have caused to stand in places of authority moving in degrees of liberty that the earth has never seen. It will be the time that you will notice the difference of administration that will be coming into My House in this hour," saith the Lord.

"I will cause a call to come forth in the earth that will bring great establishment in ways that the church has never seen. It will be a time that you will find men coming together on issues and the leadership of My Church will not be divided but they will be united," saith the Lord.

"I will cause the spirit of the patriarch to come forth in this season, and it will be the hour of the unveiling of the purposes of My Kingdom that shall come into a height in this generation that the earth has not yet seen," saith the Lord.

"I will call oppressed men out of their oppression in this season and you will find them coming into a place of understanding their purposes as they sit at the feet of the fathers in the House of the Lord. I will bring forth these fathers in the earth that will not be known by their gray hair, nor for the texture of their hair, but you will locate them by their wisdom," saith the Lord.

"I will bring the reality of the family into focus during this season. Oh! How I long for you to see My plans for this hour! It will be the day of revival coming to families in this nation and the nations around the world. I will cause fathers to have a special sensitivity. Be not deceived, for the fathers that I will bring forth will not be known by their physical strength, nor by their economic strength, but they will be known by the strength of character that I will bring forth in this hour. It will be a time of the unveiling of the characters of men that are for Me so that it will be easy to spot those that are against Me," saith the Lord.

I looked up in the heavens and I saw a river flowing. The Lord said, "Behold the River of Life" Then the word of the Lord came unto me saying, "It will be the time that I will cause the fathers to become dispensers of the life that is to come forth in the earth. You will see church fathers emerging that have will have major voices in the decades to come. Then I heard a voice coming out of the heavens saying, "Where are the fathers? Where are the fathers?" Then the Word of the Lord came unto me saying, "You are about to enter into the days that creatures above and below will come to behold this great work of My Spirit that I will do in the earth.

The days are forthcoming where you will see much revelation and mighty truths being established within My House. I will cause many creative anointings to visit thee in the earth. It will be the time where you will see the seed come forth that will bring great stress to the kingdom of darkness.

Understand this mystery! When the hearts of the children are turned towards the fathers and the heart of the fathers are turned towards the children, then I will bring incurable diseases to a halt and you will see healing beginning to flow to the nations of the earth. I will bring forth men that will not stand only as leaders, but they shall be men that will stand and be recognized as fathers within My House.

In the season of the coming forth of the fathers in the church, you will see a visitation of fathers to the nations," saith the Lord. "It will be in this season that you will find the revision of the Constitution and there will be a season of many laws that will be enforced beyond measure. Come and behold My Spirit, and you will come to know that I am a God that has all the ages in the palm of My Hand," saith the Lord.

Many of the fathers that will emerge in the church in this hour will give room for many sons to grow, and you will find enlargement and safety within My house during these seasons. I will honor the seasons of the fathers that have been latent, and I will cause them to awaken and come to full strength in this hour."

I looked upon the earth, and I saw many women with children. They were resting within the womb, and I said, "Ho! A time of many children!" The Lord said, I will cause a generation to come into place that will be shakers and movers in the earth. I will raise up men that will protect the truth of My Word, and you will see the day that I will call many individuals into a place of understanding that there has been a major change within the administration of My House," saith the Lord.

It will be the time that men will not just look for gifting in a man, but they will look to see if the character of a father is set in place. It will be the time that you will see apostles and then you will see those that will be apostolic fathers. I will show you prophets and then you will see those that are prophetic fathers. I will show you evangelists and teachers and then you will see those that are evangelistic and teaching fathers. It will be the time that you will see the difference between a leader and a father," saith the Lord.

"It will be the time that I bring the days of the kings to an end, and you will find that it will be a time of rejoicing, for I will raise up the fathers that will emerge within the land. I will bring forth mantles that will bring great correction and major adjustment in the earth," saith the Lord. "I am calling the generals in that day to be alert, and they must be watchful of the adversary that retreats back instead of advancing forward.

This will be the time you will find that men were tested in every generation, and I will cause those that have failed in the past to be a testimony for the future generals that will come into the forefront.

"I will cause you to see those that have stood and others that have failed. You will see those who have been tested concerning wealth in their day. I will cause many to be tested concerning mammon, and you will find that the testimony of mammon will be strong in this hour, but that will not be the things which will be the enemy's best for that hour," saith the Lord.

I looked up and saw the harlot, and then I heard the Word of the Lord come unto me saying, "There was a day that My servants were tested in the area of the harlot, but it will not be the ultimate test for this hour," saith the Lord. "I will cause those who have overcome to testify to My servants who will be tested in that hour. You will see the integrity of Joseph, who has stood in the house of Potiphar in his day of trial come forth with great recognition. His present struggles will become a springboard for his future achievements," saith the Lord.

Then I looked up in the sky, and I saw a hammer coming in the earth with great force. I wanted to run, and I was frozen in the place where I stood. I tried to move out of its presence, but I was mesmerized by its appearance as it hurtled towards the earth. The Lord spoke and said, "It represents great power and authority that will come into the earth." I began to rejoice, but He cautioned me and said, "Do not rejoice because of the power but rejoice because your name has been found in the book of life.

The day is forthcoming where you will see men receive great power and might, and they will become abrasive and abusive. It will be the season that I will test the generals concerning authority. I will show you those that will abuse the authority I have placed in their hands," saith the Lord.

It will be a season that a beast shall come forth out of the sea. He has a cumbersome body and horn which he used to give power unto all those that desired to receive it. I will cause My servants, the prophets, to speak against the beast that will rise up out of the sea. In this hour, you will see nations become bewitched to serve this beast," saith the Lord.

"I will expose, in this hour, the false anointing that the earth has received, and you will find that the curse which has been over many regions and the power that has ruled the region shall be broken by reason of the anointing that rests within.

Prepare thy gates and the gates of thy cities! I will give you a charge to keep out the intruders that will try to bring My people into the bondage of fear. I will cause generations that will stand in the way of that which I desire to do to depart. They will not see the day of great exploits because they would not see the promises that I was forming. Therefore, I have caused them to be moved, lest the revelation of My will blinds you."

4

The Great Emerging

"These are now the days in which I will bring about a new government within My Church. It will not be that My ways are changing, but I am causing a different priesthood which will begin to emerge," saith the Lord. "It will be the time you will see a different breed of leadership that will come forth."

I looked up and beheld a clock in the sky and I said, "What is this sign that is in the heavens?" The Lord answered me and said, "It is the hour that a different world government will emerge." I began to weep, for I beheld great persecution coming to the church. It will be the time of kingdoms that will be in direct confrontation with one another. I will cause those that have not known My Name to have an encounter with Me that they will never forget," saith the Lord.

"These are the generals that will bring forth much abundance into the earth that has never been seen by the eyes of men before. I call My people into a place of renewal, and I will speak unto thee concerning people and nations that will usher you into the next order of events which will shortly come to pass."

I saw a curtain being drawn back and the Lord began to say behold the panorama that shall come to pass in days to come. My eyes beheld a blanket of emerald green grass, and I exclaimed, "Oh! Behold! Things have changed!" I saw a cluster of trees and said to myself, "These are pleasant days!" Then the Word of the Lord came unto my saying, "I show unto you now the inward workings of man's structure." Suddenly, there appeared unto my eyes a mass of dead men's bones that were dry and brittle. The Lord began to speak unto me and said, "This is the time that I will visit the iniquities of former generations upon the present generations and you will behold My judgment in this hour." I beheld a century whose horizon opened with everything looking peaceful and desirable. It had all the signs of quality life but it was only a fabrication of good days. Then I heard the angels heralding a sound in the earth saying, "Hark! Prepare for the days of great vengeance!"

Then the bitter sounds of weeping arose to a tremendous clamor, and I saw nations that no longer possessed a sound or a distinction of their own. Then the Word of the Lord came unto me saying, "These will be the days that the Spanish speaking nations shall rise up in the earth."

I heard the distant roar of a multitude of people coming and the Lord said, "This will be the time of great marching. You will see many protests and demonstrations take place. The people that are oppressed shall begin to arise in large masses. You shall see the coming forth of major military forces in the nations around the earth.

"I will cause the 21st century to open up with major adjustments that the world has never known. I am beginning to rearrange the setting of foreign nations, and you will find governments that have been unstable in the 20th century becoming stable in the 21st century. They will become stable as they begin to seek My Face," saith the Lord.

"Now do I bring into focus the people of the veil, and you will see them rising up in great power and strength. I will cause them to be a malevolent enemy to stable nations, and you will see them moving and growing in large numbers.

The time is forthcoming that you will know the days of major religious wars. Major adjustments will have to be made. Men shall call this season, "the days of despair and agony." Women shall pray, cry and travail to their God and ask for the lives of their men.

I call heaven and earth to know My Voice in this day. It will be the time that the enemies of My Name shall become My footstool," saith the Lord. "I will cause the visitation of My Presence to be seen in the earth realm in ways the earth has never known."

I heard the Lord say, "Come! Behold the waters!" And then I saw fleets of great ships and many more ships, and I began to ask, "What is about to come forth to this generation?" The Lord answered me and said, "It is time to pray for the islands round about thee. For the days are forthcoming that I will cause many ships to dock at their shores to bring protection and safety.

The days will be forthcoming that you will find the enemy hiding in the mountains. I will cause the time of the church to come forth in ways that the church has never known. It will be in this season that you will hear of major prophetic voices coming forth in the earth. It will be the voices of those who have survived the season of the abortion age."

The voice of the Lord pierced my ears saying, "Come unto Me and I will show you the days that I will visit the dragon." I heard the weeping of their children and the Lord said, "This is the season of major change. I will bring new leadership into focus. I will cause My Church to grow, but their growth will be unnoticed until the time that I choose to unveil them. It will be the season when I will cause major voices to rise up and proclaim the gospel that will produce eternal results," saith the Lord.

"You will also see another part of the Body bringing a revelation from My Word that the church at large has never heard. I bring you into the days of shifting. The days are coming that I will shift the attention off of the western world, and I will point towards the people of China. It will be a nation that I will reach out to, for it is My will to bring them into My Kingdom. The change is forthcoming, for a generation will give their lives to the cause of My Kingdom," saith the Lord.

"I beheld the red sun, and I saw a people rising up in great power but having strong internal problems. People will be trying to flee the land, for there is coming an inward explosion. The Lord has shown unto me that, in this season, there will arise a generation of people that will not walk in the traditions of their forefathers and they will cause much bloodshed in that land. It will be a radical group, and the hearing of this report will be forthcoming in the days to come. There will be a trap set for this country, and she will lose many men by the sword. Men in high places will desire to conceal these things from the knowledge of the world, but many shall be astonished by the amount of men that shall die by the sword. Earth! O Earth! Consider thy ways! Embrace the ways of thy Creator, and you will see the days of major change!"

The Vision of the Lord continued, and I beheld the stars and the stripes. I saw a day when the flag was neatly folded and tucked away. I asked, "What has happened?" And the Lord said, "The day has come that you will see a slight change in the former flag. There will be some additions and subtractions that will be made, and its appearance shall be altered. It will be the day of developing new strategic bases for this land."

I was startled by the sound of rockets exploding in the air and the Lord said, "There will be a time of unrest in Europe as you have never seen." I heard the sound of silver and gold as it jingled in the hands of men, and that which was a god unto them shall bring them unto ruin.

"These shall be the days that those who allow their wealth to testify for their selfish desires shall hear wealth bear witness against them," saith the Lord.

Now is the hour that I will cause the people of the earth to see wonders in the heavens and upon the earth. Astounding things will appear within your atmosphere and men shall wonder at My Presence," saith the Lord. "I will cause many to stand in awe at the discoveries that will be unearthed in these days. You will behold My glory, and men shall see My Hand move in levels that will amaze them."

Then the Lord began to take me to a city that was once a place of beauty yet came to a place of despair. The Lord began to speak and say, "This place known as the Vatican shall make decisions that will affect all the governments of the earth. The church shall enter the political arena in dimensions that it could not touch in the past. It is the day that you will see the church embracing their former styles of dress that will reflect their understanding of My Kingdom, and establish firm lines of demarcation between them and the world.

Their code of ethics shall become precise, and shall be uncompromisingly enforced by the leadership of that day. The church shall come forth out of the wilderness, and recognize her authority in Me," saith the Lord. "I shall visit the religious world with a visitation of My Spirit, and this will be the time of restoration in places that many thought I would never visit again.

"Now come, and allow Me to show you the mass exodus that will take place," saith the Lord. "You will see many coming out and leaving their independent works, and many will return to the structures of the former century. The sleeping church shall come forth, for I will shake the church that once stood in the gates of its cities, and cause it to come forth in power, My glory shall move amongst them in degrees that shall thrust the deadness into light again," saith the Lord.

"Prepare! For I will cause the nations of the earth to see the changing of the hands. The nation which holds the hammer and the sickle shall become a major force within My Kingdom in the coming century. I have plans that have not yet been unfolded that you will see in these days," saith the Lord. "It will be the time that the glory of My Presence shall explode in the earth, and I will have mercy whom I'll have mercy, and show judgment upon whom I'll show judgment.

The crescent moon and the star shall be seen on the horizon, and great shall be the rise of these elements," saith the Lord. "A major war shall erupt, and rivers of blood will be seen upon the earth. I will bring division within their camps, and those that are wise shall recognize the strength of My Right Hand."

5

The Coming Forth

*I*t was as if I could look through the pages of time, and the voice of the Lord spoke unto me as a trumpet, saying, "Come and see the mighty things that I am about to bring forth in the earth!" My eyes focused on the spots of the leopard. He asked me, "Can a leopard change its spots?" And I said, "No, Lord." Then He said, "Come, and I will show you the destiny of a race that I have set within the earth.

These are the days that I am raising up a generation of people that have felt iron chains of slavery gnaw their hands and feet. Their days of oppression shall experience phenomenal growth in the century to come. In this season, there shall be a great exodus. I will show you a people that will come out of dark places, and they shall walk in degrees of revelation that was previously hidden within the earth. You will see emergence of strong men from their veil of humility that will speak to the nation at large, for they will be the new African American voices which shall speak to the consciousness of this nation. The destiny of America will be seen in this hour," saith the Lord.

The Joseph Company shall know their season, for they will be delivered out of the prison of slavery, and I will raise them up with power to become a deliverer to their nation and nations that have embraced their cause. It is the time of promotion, and the earth shall call this people forth."

These days shall see an uprising occur, and lives will be threatened in this season. I will cause war to be raged concerning racism, and you will watch Me deal with it on both sides, for it is an abominable stench in My Nostrils," saith the Lord of Hosts. "This nation will be launched into battle, and the grave dangers of this war shall cause men to embrace one another out of desperation and fear, and they will know of a new degree of unity as the nation has never experienced before. Mighty inventions shall come forth through the Joseph Company, and you will see a people that have tasted the bitter fruit of slavery come into a day of great illumination," saith the Lord. "Major discoveries in the areas of science and medicine shall come forth through the Joseph Company, and great shall be their contribution to this generation. Men shall understand My purposes as never before."

I asked, "Lord, what is the Joseph Company?" For my understanding was dim. He replied, "They who have borne the chains of oppression are called Joseph in thine ears."

The Voice of the Lord was as thunder, and He said, "Behold, the book is being opened. Read that which has been written." I saw the hourglass and beheld its sand as it was about to run out. Then I asked, "What is the meaning of all this?" The boundaries of my understanding came open, and I heard the cry and travail of Africa. I saw the burden of oppression and heard the sound of lamentations emanating from the hearts of the people. The Lord said, "I will cause the church that is within the church to begin to arise, and you will see a people that lost their land come back to a place of ownership," saith the Lord. "I shall bestow title deeds to property owners, for the earth is Mine, and I will give it to whom I so desire."

Then I heard the Voice of the Lord walking in the earth saying,

"Come forth! O children of Africa!"
"Come forth! O children of the sun!"
"Come forth! O sons of the oppressor!"
"Sit down at the tables and redistribute the land!"
"Come forth! O weeping widows!"
"Come forth! O barren wombs!"
"Come forth! Daughters of the oppressors!"
Come forth! Daughters of the free!"
"Sit down at the table… and cry out unto me!"
"Come forth! O men of dishonor!"
Come forth! O men of tears!"
"Come forth! O men of Africa!"
"Thy purpose shall be revealed!"

I was overwhelmed by that which I saw, and I entreated the Lord, "What shall happen to the land of the eagle?" He said, "In this hour, I shall bring forth the Indian nation that was exiled upon the reservations of her despot, and you will see her emerge from the murkiness of obscurity. I shall stir up the bowels of restitution, and the days are coming that you will hear of her sons claiming massive areas that have been stolen from them," saith the Lord. "Men shall be faced with the witness of deceit that shall point its finger at the greed of their ancestors.

"These will be the days that men will begin to comprehend Me as Supreme, for I establish whom I will establish, and I depose whom I depose," saith the Lord.

The earth began to rumble and shake under my feet, and I saw the sword of the Lord pierce through the sky to slay all who dared to speak against the Name of the Lord. Massive cries came forth at the judgment of the Lord. I heard the sound, as it were, of a trumpet that spoke and said, "These are the days that men who have worshipped idol gods will come to their end. Nations that had embraced the darkness of witchcraft and denied My Name shall not be in existence any longer. For I shall have them in derision... this season shall be marked with My laughter."

"These are the days that I will bring forth the seeds that came forth during the abortion age." You will see them rise up in great power and strength to bring the nations into a place of moral and correct standards of living. You will see the coming forth of their voices that will proclaim the gospel and their very lives will be at stake.

"It will be a time that the seeds which survived the abomination of the abortion crisis will become true witnesses for My Kingdom. They will be the generation that will experience martyrdom for My glory," saith the Lord. "I will cause them to possess a patience that will be phenomenal, for you will truly see My Grace abounding within them in degrees that you have never known.

"It will be in this generation that I will cause a war to erupt that will bring much defeat to the land of the eagle. Many will say, "How did we lose the war? What happened to our skill? We've never lost like this before! And then I will show you the answer," saith the Lord. "For you have carelessly killed many of your military generals during the war of abortion. The sin that has entered in this generation will have the bitter taste of quinine in the mouth of the generation that shall live in that day.

I will cause the weeping of Rachel's children to come again in the earth. For a new law will be coming forth on the medical books that will destroy newborns as they try to protect a society from a major epidemic that will come forth. It will be in this season that you will find many hiding their children as in the days of old. When this sign appears, know that My redemption draweth nigh.

"A false witness shall not be unpunished, and he that speaketh lies shall perish. For it will be in these days," saith the Lord, "that I will bring forth truth. I shall expose the men of the lies. I will show men of truth and men of lies, and you will see My Hand of judgment coming forth in this hour unlike anything that you have ever seen.

I will cause voices of major influence to speak to the medical profession. They will appear to become the new religion in the earth.

It is a plot of the enemy, but I will raise up voices that will clearly declare My purposes unto them," saith the Lord. "I will show you many mysteries, and unveil secret things in this day and hour.

I will release a cure for Aids, and you will find simple solutions to complex problems.

I will cause many to see me in a greater light than they have ever seen Me before, and I will reveal Myself in degrees that the world will not be able to comprehend, but My Church will understand Me and know who I am," saith the Lord.

Then the Lord said, "Come to the Caribbean, for I will show you the things that will shortly come to pass. I will show you the governments that will embrace stability in this hour.

I will speak to the nation of Jamaica, and I will cause them to experience a great judgment, and yet, a great revival. I will bring the church out of the darkness of religion, and you will see the economy take a new turn.

I will even cause the currency to change, and you will see a people that brought much violence within the nation experience the moving of My Hand.

It will be a season that I will bring change to the political structure that will bring massive changes in the 21st century. I will cause a new people to emerge in that land. I will address foreign forces, for the islands of the sea shall increase their independence, yet they shall experience major victories and major defeats."

I will visit an island that has a strong resource of oil, and you find them to be a people seeking the Face of the Lord. For I will move in their government and cause a tremendous awareness of My Presence to manifest in their midst. It will be in this hour that you will see My glory becoming more and more evident.

In the nation of Trinidad and Tobago, you will see the coming forth of a spiritual government, and I will establish men in high places that will become a vital force in this hour. I will cause the church of Trinidad and Tobago to come to the forefront and speak for Me. This will the day revival in that land. I will break the powers of darkness that have come to try to establish their throne in the that land, and you will see the structures of the denominational churches conferring with independent churches, and you shall see churches unite for a common cause in this nation," saith the Lord.

"I will cause a generation to emerge that will bring a radical gospel to the nation. It will be the season that the generals for the 21st century shall come forth, and you will see churches growing at phenomenal rates. You will see the weakening of major denominational bases and the rising up of a new breed of men that will affect the national political base," saith the Lord.

"I will remove the ungodly out of their seats of government, and you will see My Glory coming in a generation which the land has never seen. Come, and allow Me to work through you, for I will raise up standards against religious kingdoms that do not represent My Name," saith the Lord.

"I will return to your schoolhouses and bring back standards of education that the enemy has tried to remove. You will see Me cause a man to come into office that will bring the nation into a reality concerning seeking My Face. I will bring forth national days of prayer and fasting that will come forth through the church , and you will see the nation moving towards major spiritual trends that you have never seen," saith the Lord.

"I call you to behold the land of Barbados, and you will see the glory of My Presence arise upon the land. I will make this a spiritual base for the move of My Spirit. You shall see people coming from far and near to behold the things that I will do in this hour. A brand new day shall break forth! I will occupy the seats of government in that land, and you shall see a people coming forth in that nation which will become bread to the islands that surround her. Major voices shall come forth that shall speak to political principalities.

I will cause the economic base to become strengthened with another resource unlike anything that you have ever seen with the natural eye. I will remove the men that will try to bring greed in that land, and My righteousness shall prevail," saith the Lord. "Those that attempt to bring foreign religions on your shores shall be brought to destruction.

For the enemy has boasted and said that he would take the youth of this coming generation, of the 21st century, but I will cause a major revival that will spearhead one of the greatest moves of My Spirit. I will call the church to much prayer, for Barbados will become a spiritual capital in its region," saith the Lord.

"I will now take you to the land that has been covered with gross darkness, and you will see the lifting of the veil over the land whose flag has black on the top and red on the bottom. But I will turn the flag around," saith the Lord, and you will see My blood of rule and reign on top and darkness shall be underneath where it belongs. You will see satanic strongholds cast down by the power of My Word, and I will bring judgment to government leaders in that nation. There will be a continuous filtering of their leadership, until I shall appoint the one that is coming who will bring great deliverance unto that land.

Covenants of darkness were made centuries ago and brought a curse upon this land, but I shall destroy the curse from the root in one generation," saith the Lord. "I shall move sovereignly in this land. Oh, come, and allow Me to show you the things that I will bring forth in this hour, for the 21st century shall bring a new government in the land, and you will see their captivity begin to be turned around," saith the Lord.

There is a volcano that will erupt in an island that shall cause its land to become desolate," saith the Lord. "I will raise up strong voices that will bring a word of clarity to the islands of the sea."

Military bases shall come into great strength, and the days will come that you will see military action in the island of Jamaica. I will call forth the church into an hour of prayer and My purposes shall be fulfilled in the land," saith the Lord.

"**O**pen thine eyes and behold the judgment of the Lord that goes out towards South Africa, for this shall be the day that I will move upon the land in a way that you've never seen," saith the Lord. "It will be the season of major political changes in the government and reforms shall occur at astronomical levels. Her men shall lift their voices in the 90's, yet they will only sound for a short period of time. I shall cause many new voices to come out of her midst.

In that day, sages of great wisdom will come forth with answers that will bring the ravages of war to a standstill in the nation and across the land." I gazed upon the sea of humanity whose eyes were searching for purpose and destiny. And the Word of the Lord came unto me saying, "Come now and allow me to show you the generations that are about to come into the earth. For this will be a seed that will bring major confrontation. It will be the time that My glory shall come forth in ways and degrees as you have never seen."

I was transported again, and I saw the hot, acrid sand of a desert land as far as my eyes could see. I saw tanks of every imaginable size loom upon the horizon. The Lord began to say, "This is the hour that you will see the great change of hands. Nations whose voices were silent in the affairs of men shall break forth and become major voices in the earth. Ambition shall be their portion, and they shall attain unto great power.

This is the season that those kingdoms which seemed insignificant in the past shall come forth and be recognized. It will be the day of the gathering and the confederation of small nations. Their voices shall be heard in a major way to impact major decisions such as the earth has never seen.

> *The elevation of Spanish-speaking nations will increase and grow at phenomenal levels. You will find the voices of Spanish-speaking leaders being heard on a national level.*

It will be the day that they will hold the key of deliverance for many nations. I will cause them to emerge in such a degree that they will cause kingdoms to topple that are not rooted and grounded in My plans and purposes. I shall raise them up to judge the greed that has overtaken many nations, and they will be used to take the deceitful in their own deceitfulness.

Come now," saith the Lord, "and allow Me to bring you to France; a nation that has known much corruption and has been void of My Spirit. This will be her day of visitation, for I shall bring a two-fold visitation to her people. It will be the time that I will cause judgment to sweep the land, and I shall breathe revival into their veins, and gave them a heart of flesh. It will be the season of major changes in her government, and you will see many mighty men removed in a day, and great and powerful men raised up in a day. It will be the season I shall cause men to take note of My Presence in this nation, and they shall proclaim it to be a 'great shining forth.' I will cause a people that have known gross darkness to experience and emit a bright light. It will be the day named 'The Great Illumination.' Come! Behold My Church in that land! It will be the day of the mighty warrior, and you will see the final charge being given to this generation to carry My gospel in that land to degrees that it has never been done."

There is a time approaching that will bring a great collapse, and you will see governments that are foreign to this society come to aid governments that appear to be firmly established. I will cause the wisdom of the simple to come into being, and men will see that I am a God of promotion and demotion—I raise up, and I take down," saith the Lord.

Behold the latitude of the Lord, and you will find that the Lord will bring you into a place where there is room that has not yet even been perceived. "It is the day that I will bring forth an expression of My Presence in the land of India. A place that has been filled with gross darkness and idolatry shall experience a great shaking by My Right Hand. This will be the season of the mighty witness of My existence," saith the Lord of Hosts.

> *"India will experience a situation that will come in a populated area and bring great loss of life. Your ears shall be pierced with the mournful cries of children and parents weeping, for they have lost loved ones that were not able to escape*

My wrath. Yet, this will be the season of major reconstruction such as none has ever known.

I will cause men that have ruled with an iron hand to become halted within their tracks in many areas. You will see the breaking down of strongholds, and there will be the coming forth of a new breed that has been in hiding and is not afraid of death. Come! Listen to My Voice, and know that it is My Will to raise up a people that will have an ear for My Voice and place them for My glory.

A major event will take place in the year 1992 that will cause many to look back and reflect on this year. It will be a timepiece for many people to refer to the political changes and many people will not be in the right position to harvest according to My Word.

Behold the wisdom of the Lord in this season, for it will be the time that I shall wash away the cancer of greed in the land—it will be the hour of great cleansing. I will come and judge systems and standards that are an abomination in My Nostrils."

> *I saw the Hand of the Lord breaking out of the sky holding the money of men. He said unto me, "Look upon the money that now is, and the money that shall be." As I beheld the denominations of the bills, the mouths of the men that were on the bills began to droop, and water poured from their eyes. I asked, "Why are they mourning? What is the weeping that I hear?" The Lord answered me and said, "It is the hour of their burial, and a currency shall arise that will not remind you of these men anymore."*

Then He took me up and showed me another nation emerging out of obscurity. I asked, "What is the rise of these people?" He showed me names that I could not pronounce, and I saw the names of men that had many consonants, but the vowels were very few, if any at all. I said

"Lord, what does this mean?" And He said, "These are the people that I will begin to raise up in the land that will show forth My glory in ways that the earth has not seen. They have been hidden, but the remnant that I brought forth in their nation has become their salvation. These are the days that men shall know that I raise up nations and take down nations according to My purposes."

The sun darkened, and the clouds began a sinister dance above my head, as lightning flashed across the sky. The ominous sounds of thunder shook the fiber of my very being. And the Voice of the Lord declared, "It is the day that My Glory shall be seen in ways that shall bring forth great light into the earth." The Hand of the Lord appeared with a pen, and began to inscribe letters that fell in a pile before my feet. I noticed the markings on the envelopes that appeared to be stamps, and it was the number 30. I asked the Lord, "Isn't that the time that Jesus started His public ministry?" The Lord said, "Behold the mystery—for when you begin to see the postage lettered delivered at 30 cents, it will be a sign to the earth that I am bringing forth a breed that will be very young, but that will represent the ministry of My Son Jesus in the earth and bring conviction to mankind that will force many to fall to their knees and acknowledge Me, for I am God, and beside Me there in none other."

hen the Word of the Lord came unto me saying, "It is now the time to behold the coming forth of the voices that have been shut away in the prisons." Then I saw an angel descend upon the earth bearing a golden key, unlocking the doors of men that have been held in bondage by the world system that now exists. They were released to become voices to the system that was now about to fail. "It will be in this time that you will see the coming forth of heralding trumpets that have not been polished by the world systems, neither have they been tuned by the spirit of the age. My words shall sound through the unpolished trumpets and will pierce the shell of unbelief that surrounds many."

Mine eyes began to burn, as an acrid cloud of grey dust consumed my vision of the land. I inquired of the Lord and asked him, "What is this that has come into the atmosphere?" He replied, "It is the day that an unusual volcano shall belch a cloud of ash in its fury, forming a cloud in the atmosphere that shall obscure the vision of men, and cause multitudes to flee from the west coast. You will find air traffic increasing and the days will be seen that the ears of the sky will resound with the cries from the earth.

I looked through the tunnel of time at the close of the 20th century and saw an exchange of names in many areas. Unfamiliar companies were clothed with the fame of men. As I beheld the land of the eagle, the imposing visage of an owl emerged grasping the jewel of national prominence in its claws. The Lord said, "There is a new dynasty that will emerge within the nation but it is not the time for them to be revealed. It will be a dynasty that will bring great wealth in a seat of high office, and in the 21st century, you will see the insidious ascension of a ruling family that will almost force the nation of the eagle to embrace monarchy."

The ground began to quiver and shake, and great wealth and influence was spewed from its mouth. I cried, "Where does all this wealth come from?" And the Lord answered, "Out of the state that is known for the greatest amount of stars. I shall deliver them from the tentacles of calamity and cause minerals to spring forth that shall extricate them from the pit of despair. I shall cause them to wear the yoke of leadership in an economic wave that shall come forth in a short season in this nation."

The days will come in the nation of the eagle that a plot will be exposed, and you will see men led out of office wearing the cloak of shame. The course of election will take an unnatural turn in society. You will find that the change of government will occur shortly, for men will begin to cry out for the salvation of another system. The old order will desire to remain, yet the new guard will demand a change in their day. I will cause a form of government to sweep the land that will cause much anger and internal conflicts to seethe in the cauldron of this society, but though a generation will suffer, the following generation shall take its Sabbath rest," saith the Lord.

I looked up and saw a number system that was unfamiliar to my knowledge. The voices of men who were smug in their ways began to hiss and speculate, crying, "What is the alarm? Oh, we were looking forward for this to take place at any moment!" Their ignorance blinded their eyes to the reality of dominion, for wise are the strategies of that nation. I heard the Lord say, "I will cause a people who have multiplied themselves in your land to speak at this time in a language that you will be forced to learn. It shall appear to be sweet as honey, but the end result shall be bitter in thy bowels."

The Lion of Judah arose from His throne and proclaimed, "Wisdom, power, and strength! Come to My people that have understood My ways!" Then the Word of the Lord was trumpeted by voices that brought forth another culture and the gospel they proclaimed brought liberation to many communities.

"The days are forthcoming that you will see much immigration from Europe and nations that have not known Me into the land of the eagle. I will cause buildings that have been empty and devoid of My worship in the 20th century to reopen, and the holy sound of true worship will echo in the ecclesiastical church structure to bring a people that are looking for Me into a realm that they will be able to identify Me." saith the Lord.

"For the vessels that I shall choose will be trumpets of brass that I will painstakingly polish. They been tarnished from being exposed to the wrong atmosphere and were not used in their season of appearance. I will raise up vessels that have been neglected and put on the shelf to come down and be an expression for My glory. But I warn you not to look at the appearance of the vessel with your naked eye, for I shall bring forth men and women that are reckoned to be the dregs of society. I will cause you to know it is not the vessel, but the substance and the wind that I will cause to flow through these that I am bringing forth in these days," saith the Lord.

I looked up and saw angels upon the horizon, holding trumpets and bows in their hands. Then I saw another company of angels coming with arrows and they were dispatched to equip a generation of men. My understanding increased as the burden of the Word of the Lord burned within my bosom. "Now it is time for a generation, which shall display My Presence to their generation, to begin to prepare to wage war with a system that shall be called barbarian. A spirit, which has come out of a cave-like dwelling, shall arise and cause a cannibalistic people to come into place. You will hear of sacrifices that will be abominable in My Sight. I will bring forth men that will take the arrow of My Presence and bring destruction to an enemy, not only of My people, but to all mankind," saith the Lord. "It will be the day of the mighty warrior. I will cause the season of struggle to become a season of rest for My people, for there remains a rest that many shall experience and has not been known in the past."

I looked and saw the altars of Baal that had once again arisen in the earth to steal the affections of men from the Living God. Then I heard the torturous sounds of groaning and travail that relentlessly gnawed upon my ears, and I wept at the cries of the innocent children, and begged my God for mercy. I beheld the Face of the Lord as He beckoned me. "Begin to prophesy to the generation that will sacrifice their children to idols and say, 'O those who embrace the spirit of Baal, that once again tries to exalt yourself in the earth, destruction shall come to you and a stranger shall rule over you. For your seed has been scattered throughout the earth, and you will see again the dispersing of your seed throughout the earth. These will be the days that the coming of My judgment will be seen, and you will know that I will bring forth prophets of different orders which will warn you. This will be the day of the final warning.

You shall see the day which the flag of this nation will swing in the air, but is shall proclaim a message of grief and tragedy, rather than a message of hope and liberty. It will be in this season that one event shall follow another event, and cause the earth to wonder at the catastrophes therein. For when the flag is raised upon its pole, it will only stay up for a short period of time and then return to the depths of mourning again. It will be a season of much grief, and I will cause signals to be sent that will grab the attention of a nation which I love and have birthed to bring other nations into their purpose for the age.

I will cause the flag with the olive leaf to be unfurled, and it shall speak loudly in the skies of that land," saith the Lord. "It will be the season that the flags, who have been first in the order of things in the 20th century, shall wave last in the order of things in the 21st century. I will cause the procession of flags to come forth and in the season of the first quarter of the 21st century, you will see nations whose flags are waving that will be unfamiliar to your nation's eye, but I will do the unusual and change your allies," saith the Lord.

"Come and I will show you a people and a sound that I will allow to be trumpeted in the earth." Once again I was hurdled through the annals of time, and I saw a nation that was the seat of religion. I saw the papacy and the ornate garments which took on new meaning. Then the Lord said, "These will become voices that will be sending forth a sound to governments that have held many people in bondage. I will even raise up a new breed of leadership within their structure. They shall behold young people taking responsible positions. Behold My curious sign, for when you see the age of leadership decreasing by 10, then you will know that it is the season of war against the elderly. Nations shall be ruled by their children, and you will see young leaders emerging. I will, in this season, cause a shifting of government in major nations, and you will find that the white-haired men shall be slowly eliminated out of accepted society."

Then I heard a sound in Heaven from the mouth of the messengers. The declaration of the Word of God poured forth in the midst of travail, "O aged men and women come forth, for the generation you have forsaken has been raised up to bring you judgment, but the day of your reproach is now over. O aged men and aged women! High is the price that you have paid to allow your seeds to be trained by another, for they never learned commitment and loyalty at your hands. Bitter tears shall you now weep, for the sting of neglect shall pierce your heart as they abandon you to the cold sterility of institutions with only loneliness and regret to keep you company. I will cause you to weep and mourn, but I shall have mercy upon you, and I will pull back the covers of grief, and you will come forth into honor, for your day of reproach is over. O aged men and aged women—if only you have heard the prophet, then you would have never known the tears that are even yet pouring out of thine eyes, but take courage, for I will cause the cup of iniquity that has been laid at your door to come to an end. Wallow no longer in the quagmire of sorrow, but arise and rejoice, for the day of your reproach is now over," saith the Lord that has mercy upon thee.

"These are the days that fresh flowers shall come forth without the scent or touch of the world. They shall possess markings that shall make these unrecognizable to the naked eye. These are they who came forth from a generation that has lost its virginity to the spirit of the age. I will bring these virgins forth to be a sign to the age that I have reserved them unto Myself, for they shall keep covenant with Me," saith the Lord.

"Prepare! Generals shall appear on the horizon and they shall lead in one of the world's greatest crises. It will be the hour that you will find many generals waiting in suspense. They will sense the mystery of the hour, and great expectancy shall be their portion. There are nations whose fate has been weighed in the balance, and the terror of My Presence shall force them to their knees in repentance. This season of judgment is ordained of My Hand. Those that harden their hearts to the wooing of My Spirit and refuse to seek My Face shall eat the fruit of destruction, yet I shall abundantly bless those that seek out My purposes—they shall be as iron tried in the fire.

Fear not, My son, to behold My Will for the destiny of nations in this hour, for I shall do the miraculous and cause you to experience the judgment that I will declare unto you which you must speak into your generation," saith the Lord.

"he earth is about to experience a new degree of My Presence and I shall move sovereignly upon her. It will be the day that you will see the glory of My Presence in ways that you have never seen," saith the Lord. "I shall envelop My Church and cause an outpouring of the rains of My Spirit to fall upon her, and she will experience the move of My Spirit as never before.

I shall charge men and women with a peculiar anointing, and as they proclaim My Word, men shall feel the shaking of My power. It will be the day that great honor and recognition shall rest upon the prophet's function and will bring great glory to My Name. You will hear of prophetic voices that will speak to governments and the ministry of the statesman will become more and more evident in this hour," saith the Lord.

A cloud of mist enveloped my eyes as the vision of the Lord began to overtake me. I saw a man that was offering the sweet smelling incense of worship unto the Lord. Then I beheld the angel of the Lord branding his heart with the message of the purpose of God for His generation. I looked again and the man could not speak and I said, "Lord, why has the mouth of this priest been put to a halt?" I began to intercede and the Lord said, "The time is not yet but the days are coming that I will loose the mouth of the priest. For I have shut the mouth of the prophets until the time that I have chosen to speak through them," saith the Lord. "You will hear them prophesying My Will in the earth, and they will cause the destiny of men and nations to be made clearer, and they will articulate My purpose for the hour," saith the Lord.

"Not only will the prophet's voice echo throughout the earth, but the apostles shall demonstrate My power and authority. Churches will be established according to My divine purposes, even as the days when the first apostles walked the earth.

Divine order shall mark My House in degrees that will make the 20th century church appear ancient. I will cause a people to emerge that will show the pattern of My Kingdom to the world.

It will be the day that you will find the church taking a new level of ministry within the earth. For this is the time that I will cause My Presence to be revealed in ways that you have never known. The beginning of the 21st century will see a unique move of My Spirit whereby I will cause men and women to minister in teams. The earth shall smell the sweet incense of team ministry that will be born of covenant relationship, for the 90's are just beginning. You will see indisputable proof of My Hand in the 21st century," saith the Lord.

I looked up and saw a tree full of buds that were not in bloom, and I asked the Lord, "When shall this tree present her fruit?" And the Lord answered me and said, "In the darkness hour of the winter of 1995, I will cause fruit to spring forth and men will see My Hand in ways that you have never known. It will be the season that major voices shall emerge and sound in the land, yet this will also be the season of major departures. I shall cause a great exodus of major voices, and then I will set the new order of events in motion."

I then cried out, "Oh Lord! Teach us how to number our days so that we will know the timetable of the events that will take place." A calendar for the decade appeared before my eyes, and I heard the Voice of the Lord saying, "Sit down, and I will make things clearer and clearer through My servants, the prophets. I will cause them to become a clear voice in this hour, for the time of their emergence is at hand."

I saw the handwriting of the Lord on tables of stone and I beheld the names of generals that were about to be released in the earth. Then the Lord said, "Come and I will show you how I begin to mark My servants." I beheld the Name of the Lord in the foreheads of His servants and they became witnesses of the Kingdom. The Lord spoke yet again, "These are the days that I will cause phenomenal growth to come forth in the church, and you will see the witness of My Kingdom coming in degrees that will stagger the minds of men.

Come and allow Me to show you the things that will befall your generation." I heard a new sound in the House of the Lord, and I saw messengers coming into the earth. The ears of the anointed servants were open and they began to hear the sound and the message that emanated from the Throne. Then the Lord said, "Now is the time that you will hear men speaking a message of hope, and you will see the standard of holiness returning back into My sanctuary. For this will be the season that I will remove the priesthood of the world out of My House, and you will find them ministering in the outer court of My tabernacle. But yes! There is a priesthood you will see coming forth that will be a faithful priesthood for My glory. My judgment shall separate those that will minister near unto Me and those that will minister far, far from Me."

Then I beheld the Hand of the Lord coming down in the earth before the close of this century. I saw a measuring rod in the hand of an angel, and before I could ask "Why?" the Lord began to speak yet again. "Before I bring forth the next order of events, I must bring a pruning and purging in My Church." Then I saw the angel going to the door of every work that was in the earth. The proclamation was made as to what would remain and what would be uprooted. I cried, "Lord! Oh, mercy! Mercy! Have mercy!" He said, "Now is the time that I will remove major denominational leaders off the scene that will come to the brink of 1999, but they will not cross over into the year 2000. My ears are filled with the piteous sounds of great pleading and begging from a people that cannot discern My ways, for in their ignorance, they shall think that the enemy has transgressed My law of life when their leaders depart, and these people shall try to raise up the men that I have eliminated. O foolish and presumptuous ones, do you not realize that these men come to their reward at My Hand? I take pleasure in the death of My saints, for they have fulfilled their course for their generation. Let their souls now rest in peace."

Then I began to look up and the angels were still measuring the works in the earth. I saw financial institutions, churches, and many other places that appeared to be in order, yet the angels stopped at each door with a plumbline in their hands to measure and inspect each operation in the earth.

The Lord said, "I will choose only those things that are called to serve My purposes for the coming generation that is on the horizon." I saw works being chosen that seemed not to serve the purpose of God. Then I said, "Why would you choose things that appear to be the Goliath's of yesterday?" He said, "Some things are reserved to judge evil and others will be preserved to gather up riches to pour into My purpose." Then it was made clear to me. The voice of the Lord will begin to fill the earth saying that the wealth which the wicked has held in their possession is now coming into the hands of the righteous that are possessing His Kingdom in the earth.

Suddenly, I heard a great cry in the heavens saying, "Now is the hour of the great witness." Voices began to emerge from the depths of the sea that brought great trembling to the nations of the earth. The Lord explained, "Another kingdom is about to emerge that will cause rivers of blood to flow everywhere it goes." Then I heard the sound of weeping and wailing, and the Lord said, "I will cause the church to prepare a generation that will confront this kingdom, and they will endure hardship as good soldiers."

The ominous sight of the guillotine appeared before my eyes, and the Lord said, "This kingdom that will emerge out of the sea of nations will bring beheading of men back into society that will tremble at the cruelty of their government. They will expand for a period of 40 years, then I will bring a halt to their system, and you shall see them collapse as they face My fury. It is the season that the generation that will hear My Voice will see My power in operation, for I will cause men to occupy places of responsibility and My power will be demonstrated in the earth.

The days are coming that I will establish prophets in this nation that will carry the Word of the Lord to leaders and cause them to know which direction to move in. I will call many to respond to a crisis that will bring sorrow and weeping to a neighboring country. I will show you the island of Bermuda. I will bring forth a miraculous intervention in the midst of their extremity. It will be the time you shall see My Glory in ways that men will know that I, and I alone, have spared a people," saith the Lord.

"You will see a war that will only last for a few days and its violence shall grab the attention of the world. It will be known as the war of the great disaster. Men around the world will whisper in fear and repugnance at the evil which they shall see with their eyes. I will cause you to hear of wars on every front," saith the Lord. "Fret not, for I will cause you to know that I have everything under control.

Come away, My beloved, and allow Me to show you the coming of My Kingdom." I saw a people both great and small of all races and nationalities, and their worship was so beautiful. Then the Lord said, "Notice that I keep the distinction of each nationality, for I am a God of vast creativity. The worship that will sound in My House will be the worship of all the different nationalities that will herald the coming of My Kingdom. It is the day that you will hear the distinction of sound in the worship, and you will begin to know what each nation has been called to contribute to the beauty of My Kingdom."

The heralding trumpets began their fanfare, and I heard His Voice proclaim, "Let the procession of nations begin!" I saw nations I didn't recognize, and He said, "All that I have set in the earth will glorify My Name." I saw abilities and strengths as each nation came to process before the Lord. The Word of the Lord came unto Me saying, "Understand that this will be a sign in the earth that you are coming closer to realizing My purpose for your generation.

"Russia, O Russia, that has held the hammer and sickle in the palms of rough hands, your day has now come for you to proclaim the Word of the Lord unto the nations! These are the days that I will show the earth another sign, for when you find missionaries coming from Russia to preach on your platforms and in your places of worship,

I will bring forth a revival that will come to the earth to shake many nations into the awareness that I am a sovereign God and that I rule over the nations. Oh, you will look and think that you are being a blessing to the Russians, not knowing that I will raise them up to provoke you to jealousy," saith the Lord.

I looked over the waters and saw men, great and small, whose eyes were fixed upon the sun rising high in the sky. Then I beheld a great shinning light that came forth out of the east, as far east as one could see. Then I beheld a great company of men that was increasing and they were coming out of every nation under the sun. The Word of the Lord came unto me saying, "These are the days that you will see the present day generals passing their batons to the next flank that will arise to take leadership. Nations shall pass their batons to other nations, also. You will see nations being realigned and the realignment will not only be within nations, but I shall cause new governments to emerge that will bring great glory to some and great dishonor to others.

The days that are forthcoming will cause great waves to appear in the sea. Behold the clouds!" I saw the clouds of time rolling back and making room for a new government that was coming forth across the land. Then the Lord said, "Now is the time that you will see foreign elements coming together that will confederate and cause much irritation in the earth."

Then I beheld a gale of wind blowing into the earth that was rising at an enormous speed. I saw trees blowing about, surrendering their strength to the power of the wind, and they were uprooted and thrown about. I asked, "What is this wind bringing?" The Lord answered and said, "A mighty wind shall blow in the 21st century that will uproot many areas." I saw the eternal calendar of time and saw the year 2005. The Lord said, "In this season, you will see the shifting of many governments, for My Will must be made manifest in the earth. When you see the blowing of this wind, know that I am going to begin to establish My people in ways that they have never known. These are the days of major changes."

The Lord brought me to the windows of time, and He said, "This is the season that I will bring forth men and women who will have the understanding of time and events." I saw the first quarter of the century. I saw the skeletons and ruins of a great collapse, and then I saw a time of rebuilding and the season of great recovery. I was transfixed by the awareness of the vision, and I heard the Word of the Lord say unto me, "Come and prophesy concerning the years to come." Then the Lord said, "I will cause man to come into office who will bring great hope to that nation, but the action and turning of things will happen slowly. Take heart, for it will surely manifest.

Come and allow Me to show you the Church." I saw a people coming out of hiding that was greatly persecuted for what they believed. I saw a mighty army coming forth, but this time it was not with military, but great spiritual force. "These are the days that you will see a leader who will cause the stirring of recovery in your midst," saith the Lord.

The heavens opened, and I beheld torrents of rain falling round about me. I was astounded as the Lord said, "Come and see the new thing that I am doing, for in this generation I will cause a visitation of the rains of My Spirit that will bring a strong prophetic wave amongst My people. They shall shake nations with this anointing, and will bring foreign elements to their knees. That which you will see come forth in the mid-nineties will only be a seed compared to that which I will bring forth in the next generation. I will cause men to emerge that shall bring a great accusation against kingdoms that have not represented My purposes."

I saw an abundance of coins, and was mesmerized by their hypnotic glitter. I shook my head in amazement, totally bewildered by what I saw. The Lord said, "You will see a run on coins unlike anything you have ever known in this season. When you hear of the run on coins, know that this will be the season of economic strains. But it will also be a time that you will see the coming forth of a mighty spiritual wealth of increase in the earth. You will see My Hand in ways that you have never seen. Prepare for visitation, for I shall be glorified," saith the Lord.

11

The Word of the Lord for the Third World and the Nations Surrounding the Caribbean Sea

The Word of the Lord came unto me saying, "Now is the time to behold the mighty work that I will be doing in the nations that have been in obscurity, for a generation that has been hidden from view shall now be propelled into the forefront. I shall reveal My eternal purpose in the year of 1992, and this shall be the season known as their unveiling."

I felt my eyes begin to burn as the fire of the Spirit enveloped me, and the Lord continued to speak and said,

"Behold Cuba! This is the season that I will visit that nation and cause it to be redirected and it shall fulfill My purpose in this hour! It will be the season that I will cause the guards to be changed, and you will see things begin to change their present course in dramatic and enormous way in and around the year of 1994. You will behold the hour that I will cause changes in nations with which they have economic interaction.

It will be the time that they will form new alliances. The events shall stagger the world, and you will see that My Grace is ever present."

The angel of the Lord began to point my eyes towards the Bahamas, and the voice of the Lord continued to speak. "Look at the Bahamas! Behold a land that appears pleasant upon its surface, yet within its structure there is great economic tension seething as molten lava awaiting its time to explode into view." As I stood gazing, there was an unearthly clamor that began above my head, and I saw a strange creature hovering in the sky. An eagle soared in from the north of the creature and began to screech a song of urgency, "The time is now! The time is now! The time is now!" I spoke unto the eagle and asked, "Oh, eagle! Oh, eagle! What time is it?" The eagle refused to answer, and flew away in disgust. The creature began to scream out, "Change! Change! Prepare for changes in currents on every level, for the Lord God Almighty has spoken it."

The creature flew away, and the waters began to churn in response to the Presence of God. I heard the Voice of the Lord declare, "The days of the nations that have exploited thee are now coming to an end, and I will remove the spirit of greed out of your midst.

A very militant church will emerge at this time," saith the Lord. "I bring it forth in the next generation." As I saw the panorama of events unfold before my eyes, I saw people dressed in uniforms. Before I could voice my query, the Lord answered my curiosity and said, "This will be the time that I will turn the education systems over into the hands of My people and many shall come from far and near to learn My ways. Prepare for changes and voices that will bring alteration to the complexion of its present systems."

I saw a spotted animal move stealthily across the land. Then the Lord said, "Can a spotted animal of this nature change its spots?" and I said, "No." Then the Word of the Lord came unto me saying, "Surely thou shalt see the eternal metaphor, for this is the time that you will see a country rise in great independence and influence from nations outside of herself." I beheld jewels, wealth and resources that was coming from a far away land. Then I saw hordes of people returning back to this nation that had departed earlier during its humble beginnings. The Lord spoke and said, "I will cause a great rebuilding and modernization to take place. It will be the season that I will send wealth from afar. The days of tainted money will be over and it will be the days of pure money that will come forth in your systems."

The angel of the Lord took me by the hand and caused me to ascend into heavenlies. I heard the Word of the Lord say, "Come and allow me to show you the land of the poor and the rich." I wondered, "What kind of land can this be?" I heard sounds of prayer and intercession coming out of the land of Puerto Rico. Another angel came out of the heavenlies and I saw a golden cup filled to the brim with wrath and indignation. The Voice of the Lord thundered and said, "I will come and judge the idolatry that has existed in the high places of this land. It will be the hour that you will see the coming forth of My Church that will speak against the forces of witchcraft, and I will cause those that sought to ascend into places of power through these means to be removed in devastating manners in years to come. I will show this land that I am God and beside me there is none other."

Then I heard a major shift in the sound of the winds and the Lord said, "The days of illegal drugs will come to a height within this decade and I will raise up a man that will affect the nation and bring forth shock waves of power. It will be the season that you will hear the sound of laughter in the heavenlies, for I shall laugh in derision at the plans of the enemy. I will cause mighty men to come forth in this hour and they shall bring salvation to this nation.

I shall also touch their water supply and you will behold My doings. It will be the season you will see the unfolding of My purpose and the time will come that you will find I am a God that brings mercy to whom I will bring mercy," saith the Lord.

I saw the island of St. Thomas, and I saw a nation that was called upon at this hour to guard its borders and prevent foreign gods from entering their land. "It will be the time that I will cause things to tighten at your borders," saith the Lord. "It will be the season that you will hear a sound of repentance and revival sweep the land. I will cause a church to emerge within the nation that will experience phenomenal growth, and I will have the church in St. Thomas to know that there is to be no separation of church and state, for I desire to make you a prototype of My Kingdom in the island that I established you.

I will come into St. Croix and visit the denominational churches that rest within that land. You will see a day of visitation coming in your direction," saith the Lord. "It will be a time of regathering, and I will cause a new people to emerge in influence within that nation. It will be a day that I will bring wisdom unto a government that will seek My Face concerning the change of direction which I am bringing forth. It will be the day of visitation unlike anything that you have ever seen. I will cause the seasons towards the end of the 90's to bring you into a time of great laughter and joy. I will cause the economic pressures to ease, and you shall know that I, the Lord thy God, have heard thy prayers on high."

Then the Lord began to speak concerning St. Maarten. "It will be the season that the voices of healing will sweep the land, for there are men that I am raising up within the land that will bring healing to the whole man, body soul and spirit. I saw works spring up in the island and many healed by the power of touch. It will be a season of mighty renewal. These are the days that you will behold the coming together of My purpose."

There is a season of an abundance of rain by My Spirit that shall deluge the land," saith the Lord. "A foreign force will try to come in to obstruct the move of My Spirit, but I shall raise up voices that will cause it to be brought to a halt. I will cause a move of My Spirit to come in the government that will cause them to be receptive to My men servants in the land," saith the Lord.

"I will cause a wave to come to the shores of St. Kitts that will bring forth a season of clarity to a nation that has been experiencing coldness and semi-darkness. I will cause the wealth that has flowed in and out of that nation to come into My sanctuary for the purposes of My Kingdom," saith the Lord. "It will be the season that the wealth of the wicked will find its way into the hands of the righteous for righteousness sake."

I heard a cry in the heavenlies, as the voice of the Lord rang out, saying, "Oh inhabitants of the land of Aruba! It is the hour that I am calling you out of your places of darkness and into My great Light! For it is the season that you must prepare for major confrontation. I will bring about a great unveiling of the hidden works of darkness that have been taking place in former generations.

I will cause a dynasty that had great influence in the land to be sovereignly uprooted, and men will see the works of My mighty Hand," saith the Lord. "Oh, inhabitants! Hear the Word of the Lord! Prepare for the places of darkness to become places that I will show forth the light of my purpose which will bring a banquet of illumination to a people that have tasted gross darkness."

I heard the sounds of weeping and wailing that caused me to hold my ears to silence the horror of pain. The Lord spoke and said, "There is a spirit in Antigua that has tried to bring a massive amount of blood-shed in the land." I heard the heavens sending forth an alarm saying, "Pray! Pray! For the hour of prayer shall come upon you! It will be the season that I will call for watchmen in the nations to be in a season of prayer, for a place that has known My beauty will become desolate if My people do not come to their posts of prayer," saith the Lord.

Then I saw a mass of winged creatures darken the sky with their presence. The Lord said, "It is the hour that I will bring destruction to powers that have been lodging in your high places. I will bring major principalities to their knees so they will know that I am a God that rules and governs the nations."

Then I came to a land of peace and rest. I saw her name written upon the horizon—St. Lucia. The Word of the Lord came unto me saying, "This is a land that will experience a new wave of My anointing. They shall drink deeply of the new wine that I shall pour, and I will bring them into a time of great peace. Many shall run to this land because it will become a haven of rest and a place of refuge to those that I will send in their direction."

Then the Word of the Lord appeared concerning St. Vincent. There was an ominous air round about me, and I felt the hairs on my arms and the back of neck respond to the fear of the Lord. "Heed My warning!" saith the Lord. "I am calling the church into an awareness of My purpose, for I desire to bring you out of the tradition of yesterday and bring you into the reality of My Presence for this hour."

I was transfixed by the majesty of the Lion of Judah that sat upon the Throne, and I heard a roar that caused the land and the waters to tremble. The earth responded to the Presence of God and began to quake under my feet. The command of God sounded as a trumpet. "Pray for the volcanoes, for it is the time that I will call forth a people in the earth to speak to the volcano named 'Turmoil.' They must call forth peace so that it does not erupt in this generation.

Come now, and watch Me remove the ungodly that have settled at your shores, for I have a people in this land that I will keep preserved if they will hearken to My voice," saith the Lord.

As I looked upon the land of Grenada, I saw dogs fighting in the streets. Then the Lord said, "Pray for the unrest that will come to visit this nation before the close of the century. I will cause streets that were once lit to go out in a day, for this will be a season of total confusion."

I came to another place, and I heard men sitting around a table trying to strategize economic stability. Then the Word of the Lord came unto me saying," This nation shall experience a season of great economic pressures from outside forces. But I will warn this nation that they're not to compromise with the enemy, for he comes to the nation seeking to destroy the youth in the land. I will call for repentance from forefathers that have made covenants with darkness, and I shall cause the curse to become invalid in this generation. Come away to a secret place so that I can speak to thee and reveal My dark sayings."

The sounds of many religions created a miasma of worship in Guadeloupe. In the midst of the sounds I heard the wailing of the wind as it swept through the land. I asked the Lord, "What is this wind that is blowing?" The Lord answered and said, "It's a wind of purification. I am calling for a refocusing in the nation. It will be the time of major adjustments that will be called upon to see the hand of stillness. It will be in this season that I will call for light to bring clarity to thoughts and modes of thinking. I will cause churches that have tried to emerge to give birth to a church that will surface in the beginning of the century that will shake the nation with My power and anointing. There will be much migration to this land in this season.

Now is the time for visitation in the island of Curacao. As the Lord declared His purposes, I looked up in the sky and saw a dragon breathing out threatening blasts of flame from his nostrils. Then I pondered, "What meaneth this?" Then I saw beasts coming out of the midst of the sea, and the Word of the Lord came unto me saying, "Now is the time that you will hear of the pulling down of major strongholds as you have never seen. It will be the season that you will see My mighty Hand and the right Hand of My power.

This will be the time that you will hear a mighty roar across the land. It shall be the roar of despair, for the curse of poverty will try to sweep the land. I will cause the desolate places to witness the deceit of the rich, and mighty forces will come out of the places of despair to lift up a mighty standard for My Name sake," saith the Lord. "I will cause you to see the hour of great relief in the days to come, and you will experience a mighty restoration."

I saw a banqueting table set for 12 people upon a land that had known great disarray. Each place setting had dishes and goblets of gold which sat upon a white linen tablecloth. As I marveled at the beauty of the table, four angels descended suddenly upon the four corners of the table, and tossed the place settings in the air. I watched in dismay as that which appeared orderly was transformed into great disorder. I heard the Word of the Lord declare, "Haiti, O Haiti! Thy government leaders are tumbling from their places, and a new leader called 'mulatto' is emerging from the murkiness of obscurity. I shall provide a pathway for this leader to walk in, and many shall wonder at this one's ascension in that hour. Great shaking! Great changes! Great wondering at My doings in this land," saith the Lord.

"The hour has now come that you will see the island of Martinique come to a place of tremendous shaking," saith the Lord. "It will be in this season that you will feel the trembling under your feet, for the earth shall feel the impact of this hour. I will bring a cup out of this island that will be filled to the brim. It will be the time of the cup and saucer in the land. I will cause the top of the cup to spill over into the society of its day. It will no longer be a time of great separation but a time whereby they shall emerge as one in the land. I will cause a shout of anger to sound out of the heavenlies, and you will see a time of major revolving in the land.

Come forth, Martinique! The time of your freedom has now come. It is the time to come forth with the principles of My Word and My Kingdom, else you will experience bondage from the hand of a tyrant," saith the Lord.

As I looked up, a time piece came forth from the sky that appeared to be an hourglass. I beheld a hand reach out of the cloud to snatch back the hourglass from the atmosphere of the earth. The Lord said, "I shall cause time to stand still concerning St. John, for their prayers have ascended on high. It is the season that I will cause many earth-shaking speakers to come forth in the generation that is approaching, and you will see the hour that I will remove the religious seats out of the land and establish bases where I can move freely," saith the Lord. "Prepare for the hour of transfer, for it will bring deliverance to those that will find safety in this land."

Then the voices of judgment began to declare truth out of the heavens saying,

> *"Murder! Lies! Deceit!" and the finger of God pointed towards Columbia. The angels were given their orders to prepare the land for the wrath. "Destruction and devastation to a place that has hidden the dirty works of the enemy! I will cause a war to emerge in the land, and artillery will begin to surface from its place of hiding."*

"The military hour is upon you," saith the Lord. "I will raise up men in this hour who will enter that land to strengthen the church, and you will see a people that will address the problem of that nation," saith the Lord.

> *"It will be the season called the great explosion, for a bomb will be dropped bringing death and destruction such as has not been seen before upon their soil."*

I heard generations crying out under the Throne of God, for their entrance has been cut off from the earth. You will see a foreign force come to lend help, and that which appeared to be an easy prey will become a thorn in the side of the eagle in the century to come," saith the Lord.

I was summoned by the Spirit of the Lord to appear in the courtroom of judgment. The nations were aligned and murmuring, "Why are we assembled here today?" Then the judge stood upon His feet and said, "You are here to witness the divorce of nations that have stood together within old covenants."

> Then I saw a sword sever the ties between Colombia and Venezuela, and the Lord said, "I am serving a bill of divorce between nations so that My strategy can be seen in this hour, for it is the right and privilege of Almighty God to tear them asunder."

I looked and beheld walls being erected, and the Lord said, "New walls shall emerge in the century to come, for it will be the time of severing the tares from the wheat among the nations. Greater laughter shall be heard in this season," saith the Lord.

> "Nicaragua! Nicaragua! Nicaragua!" This was the name that I heard sounding out of the heavens as they were calling for "Change! Change! Change!" Then the Word of the Lord said, "Seal up the book, for the time is not yet to utter all of My purpose. The hour is now coming that forces that have been in control will wane and a young, vibrant commander shall surface for a season to take charge and lead a nation into great conflict, yet bring about major turning."

Yellow traffic signs appeared in the airways of the sky announcing a detour. The Word of the Lord came unto me saying, "The hour is now coming where you will see the air traffic rerouted in the decades to come, for I will change the international ports. It will be the time that airlines shall emerge with strange colors and names which are unfamiliar and difficult to pronounce. It will be the hour that strange writings will fill the skies and loud colors shall preen their plumage in the eyes of the nation. They shall sweep the air with their presence, and it will be the final changing of the guards that will close out the 21st century."

As I continued to marvel at the Word of the Lord, an olive leaf fell from the sky. He said, "When you see the olive leaf fall from the sky, you will see the downfall of an entire region. I saw flames of fire as judgment came to a nation."

The Lord has commanded this volume to be closed. He spoke one last time and said, "Record the mystery of the eyes, for I unveil it before My people. Many will think it strange that I speak unto My prophets, and many will doubt the validity of My Word. Great is the ignorance of the scorner, for do you not know that I set eyes within every nation to see My plans, purposes and handiwork in the earth? These are they with an eye for destiny, and I call them to be seers that shall discern My movement in the earth. These are they whose eyes are anointed with eye slave, and unto them have I given peripheral vision to see that which surrounds them - they can see in all directions. I am the Lord God, thy Creator, who shall question My ways in the earth?"

Part II

IN DEDICATION

his book is dedicated to Joshua Nathaniel Jordan, my firstborn male child who will carry the mantle of his father to future generations.

NOTE FROM THE AUTHOR

This is the third book of the *Written Judgment* series. I am under the commandment of the Lord to release these prophecies as a five-volume set. As the Written Judgment series progresses, it has been a literal sign and wonder as we witness the unfolding of the Word of the Lord on both national and international matters.

This particular volume is both sober and exhilarating. Sober... for some of what the Lord has revealed demands that we sit still in His Presence, and think on the ways of men that have caused such devastation to be birthed into the earth. Exhilarating... for God is going to show Himself mighty in long-standing situations, and He is about to empower the Body of Christ in a miraculous way.

There will be some who read this book with the eye of a skeptic— seeking to bury their head in the sand to ignore the vivid realities of God's indignation. Others will take the Word of the Lord lightly, ignoring the warnings and instructions thereof. To them, I send blessings, for God will defend His own Word.

But for those who are sensitive to hear what the Spirit of the Lord is saying, this book will prepare you for the next move of God in the earth. It will prepare your heart for endurance, and strengthen your hands for the work. I will prepare the Church for the coming visitation that shall leave people in a state of astonishment, baffled by the manifestations of God.

Let the intercessors read this, and awaken to the task at hand, for the Word of the Lord must be nurtured by the prayers of the righteous. Let those who name the Name of Christ embrace that which the Lord is saying, and be attentive to His voice, for He is God, and beside Him, there is none other.

12

Global Adjustments

The Word of the Lord came unto me saying,

> *"You have entered into the days of major adjustments, both nationally and internationally. This will be the time where you will see the process of public election take a turn for the worse, and many will be silenced during this season. The instability of nations that appeared to be so stable in the 90's, will become an overt sign to all that I am God,*

and beside Me, there is NONE OTHER."

The Word of the Lord thundered from the heavenlies, crying, "Redemption! Redemption! Redemption!" I began to wonder what was taking place as I heard the rush of angel's wings and great activity sounded from above. The Lord began to declare that this is the hour that He will cause men and women to recapture land and territories that had fallen out of their hands. They shall possess the land once again.

These will be days that you will behold the trail of tears in reverse order. For the Lord has declared that the time of the lease is about to expire, and you will see land coming into the hands of descendants who maintained a tenacious hold on the land through the Spirit, refusing to bow to the connivings of men that attempted to divest them and their family of their rightful inheritance.

Suddenly, mine eyes beheld an enormous hourglass that plummeted down through the sky. An angel began to herald, "The sands of time are running out!" I feared the seriousness of this sign and beseeched the Lord, asking, "Why has the hourglass appeared in this season?" The Lord replied, "I am beginning to change the course of nations that have stood in the forefront. For this is the day that I will come to your planet and shift the course of governments.

Prepare! A new day is about to appear! I open your eyes, and you will begin to see wars in the heavenlies." Immediately, my eyes were empowered to behold fightings and principalities in major conflict. The Lord continued to declare, "It will be the season when you will see a people emerge out of the murkiness of society with a standard that will far exceed the ethics of former generations."

Japan

The Hand of the Lord began to rest upon me as He said, "Watch the hourglass again." The Lord took my eyes as far east as I could see, and I beheld Japan in a whirlwind of change. I saw rebellion visit her soil. The Lord said,

> *"This will be the season where the youth of the nation shall be enticed by the spirit of rebellion, and they shall bring their parents to their knees.*

This visitation comes in a season that I have designed to tear down her idols that refused to acknowledge Me in their midst.

This will be a season of great upset as My judgments manifest in their midst. You will even see a seven year war waged that will astound the very soil of Japan.

This will be the season of great cups of bitterness that must be ingested by those who lacked an appetite for My Grace.

The clouds began to gather in the skies and take counsel one with another. The rumblings of their speech baffled me, and I asked, "Lord, what hour is this?" A jumble of golden letters appeared before my eyes, jumping into place to spell out their message. Yet I remained confused, for I could not understand their pronunciation. Then the Word of the Lord came strongly and began to declare, "I will change your international ports. I will raise up a generation that will refuse to compromise. These will be the days that you will see the alienation of nations that will refuse to cooperate with the nations that possess the keys of power.

The days are forthcoming that you will see a new monetary system emerge. It will be birthed in a cycle of great abomination. I will take currency that has not glorified Me from nations that were devoid of My Presence, and place it into the hands of men that will be willing to bear My Name upon their lips. I shall cause large amounts of gold to appear upon their tables, for I shall finance righteousness in the earth.

I will raise up nations that will return to the old standard of judgment. I will cause mothers to weep for their sons who have walked down the gloomy halls of oppression. For a spirit of murder will disguise itself with the mask of accusations, trials, and sentences to kill off the undesirables of society. This will occur in a season that free press will be silenced in the land. The days are forthcoming and is now that men will be hauled into places of unjust judgments because of the knowledge that they possess."

As the heavenlies grew silent, my ears began to detect the gurgling sounds of the waters of the earth. Then the Lord said, "Come to the sea of time and begin to wash your face." As I stooped down to peer into the sea of time, I began to see images in the water with tears in their eyes. I beheld the fish of the sea moaning and crying as they grieved over the carelessness of mankind that poisoned their place of habitation in the earth. The Lord said, "Because of the greed of man, fish will slowly be removed from man's diet because of the illness that will judge a society that polluted without regard for life."

As I began to walk away, I saw entire arrears of commerce come to a sudden end. Men running in circles, saying, "How did this come about within a day?" Then the Lord began to stand in the panicked faces of men and judge entire corporations for the upset and tilt that they brought to society.

Alaska

I was taken to Alaska, and I beheld a change in governments that have danced with corruption. I began to witness contracts of greed being signed, and generations unrighteously exploited. Then I saw the Hand of the Lord touch this region with shakings and quakings that continued to increase as His wrath expressed itself in their midst. The Lord began to laugh in derision at the futile attempts of scheming men to ignore His doings in their midst, and He said, "Watch me protect the innocent ones within this region and chase out adversaries in the face of this calamity!"

North America

An angel appeared, and I was apprehended by the power of God. I was in the heavenlies, and the angel cried, "The masses are coming! The masses are coming from across the waters! The masses are coming and shall fill the continent of North America! The masses are coming!" I saw people swimming form afar and traveling by sea to escape the change of government that is coming from abroad. The Lord began to speak and said, "Prepare again for a visitation of corruption to visit and expose the wickedness of the nations of greed. You will see refugees escaping the murderous hands of an angry despot who will have sold their infants and killed off their elderly. The bowels of compassion shall be stirred in the earth for the masses who are coming to escape the sadistic evil that has arisen within their borders."

South America

The Word of the Lord began to fill my mouth, and He said, "Son of man, prophesy to the powers that be." I began to open my mouth, but words would not come forth. I stood in amazement as I vainly tried to speak. Then the instructions of the Lord came forth and said, "Speak to the powers in a language that they can understand." I began to prophesy in another tongue that was unlearned to my natural mind.

I heard the dismal sound of people weeping and howling within the nations of South America. The Word of the Lord came unto me saying, "I have visitation scheduled for this people. Prepare! The land is about to regurgitate its corruption! The blood of the innocent that has spilled into the earth cries out for my judgment in their midst! I saw people rioting in the streets and entire governments collapsed overnight.

I looked and saw a large table set before my eyes. I perceived it was the table of nations. As I approached the table, I saw instead of plates, a book at each setting which represented each continent. I desired to open up the books, but I became disturbed at the action of that day. Then the Word of the Lord came unto me saying, "I will not allow you to peek into the continent of South America, but it will be a day of visitation that will sweep literal millions towards My Presence. You will see revival sweep over that land and cause many to be filled with My Spirit and abandon the vain traditions of men."

South and Central America

"But there is a season forthcoming in which I will cause the books to be opened for you to see the visitation that will come to the continents of South and Central America. It will be the day that I will expose the exploitation that has taken place and show you My glory in degrees that you have never seen before. This will also be the day that I will expose the counterfeit and the false anointings that are sweeping the earth.

The Day of the Lord will come quickly unto My people. Those that will have a hunger to know Me and follow hard after My purpose will begin to know My manifested Presence. This will be the day that I will cause men that desire to be fishers of men to walk in a level of holiness and awareness of My doings that will bless and astound the multitudes.

The Spirit of Awareness that will come upon these men and women will bring forth a level of discernment that will expose the lies that have come into the earth disguised as My anointing. I will cause men that have sought for fame in the wrong places to come into a season of great shame in the year 1999.

These are the days that I will pull off the mantles that have chosen the way of compromise and will cause a new breed of voices that will sound forth in this hour. I will cause men and women that have paid the price of isolation and endured the painful season of unpopularity to come forth from the other side of the desert. This is the season that I will make men and women that will be willing and obedient to speak My Word to stand boldly against unrighteousness.

Avenging the Oppressed and the Poor

"My Spirit shall come upon hand-picked individuals and they will prophesy against systems and laws that have been legislated to commission the demise of the oppressed. I will cause major prophetic institutions to emerge.

Prepare for war! Prepare for war! I will open your eyes to see the sleeping giants within the Church come to a place in this hour where they will cry out against the systems of oppression. For I shall so order events that none shall be able to deny My displeasure, for it shall wax hot in thy midst. He that hath an ear will hear what I am saying, and shall stand on the Lord's side.

I will stamp My foot upon those things which have fostered the confidence of men. The weight of My glory shall shake those things which men have thought were stable. Prepare for financial ruin to topple those institutions who sought to gain profit from the destitution of the poor. I will cause entire city governments to come to naught before your eyes. I will place My hand upon the lowly and cause them to succeed and beat the odds that were set by those who gambled for their demise. I will become incarnate with the poor, and you will find that those who bless them will prosper in the turn of the century. I will redefine the purpose of My Church within the earth in this hour. The Church has closed their ears and shut their eyes to the lowly, but in this hour, I will raise up a new flank of leadership that will bring forth a new definition of the role of the Church in this hour. It will not be a new Church that has never been seen before, but a Church that will move back to the biblical standard that I set up in the beginning. I will raise up men and women that will be touched with the feelings of the infirmities of men.

Prepare—for a day of laughter is coming to the earth! I will openly mock the gods of this world, and strip them of their presumed nobility before the eyes of men. My glory shall overthrow the idols of men. They shall be consumed with the cravings and lust of own hearts. When these days come, men will ask, 'Are these drunk?' and I will answer them through the voice of My servants, 'Yes, but not as you suppose.' In this season, I will bring major economic collapse and very large institutions shall fold up and close their doors quickly; they'll disappear overnight."

America

As I glazed down on America, I saw the eagle gather her wings, and rise from her place of habitation. It began to take to the sky and soar. I stood and watched until I saw the eagle no longer. I asked men who stood nearby, "What happened to eagle?" They responded, "What eagle?" and I wondered if men beheld what I beheld.

> Then I realized that I was talking to a generation that was years into the 21st century. I beheld a strange currency in my hands and centers of commerce were already changed.

And the Voice of the Lord began to speak, "This will be the day that your ports will change and you will see a people controlling borders. They did not come forth in the 20th century, but they shall emerge in the 21st century."

Genocide

I saw genocide erasing the lives of society's undesirables. It will be a day of attack upon the poor. Yet God will show forth signs and miracles for those that will run to their rescue. The days of concentration camps are quickly approaching and men are pulling out their hidden agendas. Leaders who claimed to be "for the people" will sell out the very people that the world thought they would represent.

Election 2000

God also showed me that election 2000 will bring a lame leader into office. He will be a leader who will be incapable of standing upon principles and ethics, for he will lack the strength to walk upright.

God will visit the office of the presidency with infirmity and cause the nation to begin a prayer gathering. He will expose the things that will be hidden and cause a spirit of illumination to sweep the land. Prepare, for the season of power will increase and men will pay any price to obtain the sweet mastery of success.

The Lord said, "Prepare—for the scales are descending to the earth to judge the sins of men. This will be the hour that you will hear of many false alarms concerning The Coming of the Lord. I will visit quickly, but not in the way that the earthly mind projects," saith the Lord. "There will be large gatherings, and you will see men and women running to places where they are led to believe that they will find Me, but I will not be found of them.

"This will be the hour that I will push the forerunners to the side and bring a new cabinet of pioneers to the forefront. I will cause men to come into a new place of consecration in My Presence, and I shall reveal Myself unto them. I will be found among those that hunger and thirst after righteousness, and surely they shall be filled.

These are the days that you will find men earnestly calling upon the Lord, seeking salvation on many levels. Those who have relied upon the economy of men to carry them over will come to a day of great weeping and upset, for they will find that the arm of flesh is fragile, indeed. I am preparing a day that men will see the bottom come out of economic structures that appeared so stable and investments that guaranteed definite returns will see the judgment of My Right Hand."

Then the Angel of the Lord invited me out to the sea. As I stood upon the banks of the ocean, I beheld the waves crashing against the sands. And the Word of the Lord came unto me saying, "Behold the movement of the water… for you are coming into the era that I will once again change the course that the water will be taking. You will hear My Voice within the nations that will lead in commerce and see my judgment upon those that will fall behind." Then the Hand of the Lord came upon me and set me down in the midst of the waters. I saw ships both large and small rerouted in directions they didn't want to take. But this is the season that you will see Me moving," saith the Lord, "and

> *I shall cause nations that were not able to profit in the 20th century to lead in productivity during the 21st century. This season comes so that their children may harvest the seed that their parents sowed for their liberation."*

Then I heard the Voice of the Lord saying, "Come away, son of man!" It was as if I was being lifted to a height in God which I had never known before. Then the Lord took me to the altar where the souls of men were laid, and He said, "I want you to hear the sound of voices that never had expression in the earth. I heard the lamenting voices of children who had been denied their entrance into the earth as they mourned and called for God's judgment. The Lord said, "I am about to judge men who sit in high places that have welcomed a visitation of death in the earth to suit their own corrupted and perverse ambitions. I shall answer the visitation of death with a visitation of judgment upon a generation that has removed the seed of life from out of the earth."

There was a rumbling and a shaking, and a mighty wind that began to blow. It was as if I were in the midst of a tornado, and the winds spewed me into a hall of clocks and windows. The word of the Lord came unto me saying, "Welcome to the windows of time, for I will show you the future that will shortly come to pass." As I gazed through one window, I beheld the elderly standing with tears in their eyes, looking frail, hopeless and bound. Then God said, "New laws will be passed to eliminate the elderly beyond their control and will." I asked the Lord, "Why?" He replied, "A day of recompense is coming their way, and you will see the elderly lose the right to life just as they denied that right from the seed that had no voice."

The Medical Society

I saw a panorama of diseases sweep the lands of the earth, coming out of nations that lost control of their population. Then the word of the Lord came unto me saying, "Prepare!

The day and the hour is forthcoming that I will settle issues among men and bring judgment upon the medical society. Diseases shall be rampant and out of control. They shall laugh in the faces of doctors whose efforts shall be futile against their power.

I will decrease the population of the nations, but this time, not by their choice, but by My choice.

I looked up and saw laughter in the heavenlies that smothered the sounds of the cries of men who have been victimized by a peculiar disease that will judge their refusal to repent of their wickedness. The Lord said, "Because men have refused to repent, a sexually transmitted disease will be released in the earth that shall avenge the perverseness of the appetites of men. This disease shall claim lives within months of its contagion. I will bring that which is even more frightening and deadlier than AIDS, and cause men to know that I have condoned sex only within the marriage bed. This plague shall awaken men to righteousness, and many shall call upon My Name in desperation, for there will be no help from the medical profession."

The day of the Lord will bring much upset and disgust as the coming century approaches. He said, "It will be the season that I will begin to separate those that are with Me from those who are against My plans and purposes. I will cause a transition to come forth in the leadership of the 21st century. You will see the day that the Church will have a more prominent position within society. I will cause kingdoms to be subdued by the Name of my Son. When men shall see the One whose Hands they pierced, they will come to an awakening that they must bow to the Name of Jesus."

Astronomy and Falling Elements

"I am coming in your midst as a Mighty Man of War in the 21st century. You will taste of a season of great loss upon the planet. You will also begin to hear of elements falling out of the heavens upon the earth. When you see this, know that it is the beginning of sorrows. I will cause the astronomers to be amazed, and many shall be mesmerized as they gaze into the heavens during this season. I bring men into a state of watching and beholding My Glory, for it shall be revealed and fill the earth with much pleasure.

Now is the time that I will cause the prophets within the earth to begin to stand upon their watch and see what I will do to those that will come to know My Name. This will be the season of great unveiling, and you will see the prophets proclaiming judgment upon a malevolent system that has caused great discontent. I will cause many to look for the purpose of the Lord within this hour. I will bring a new understanding of holiness, and you will hear things magnified out of the Word that men have overlooked. This will be the day of the unveiling of those things that are presently hidden from the eyes of men."

Then the Lord appeared unto me and said, "Come to the place where the horses are standing." I smelled an abundance of sickly, sweet flowers, and was shocked to behold a funeral cortege led by a lone horse carrying a body upon its back. I thought that the Lord had taken me backwards to unveil something from the past, but when I got to the calendar, I realized that the Lord was taking me into days that the earth has never known before.

A bitter cup shall be passed to a generation of brightness and brilliance. A cup of vast dregs shall be placed in front of men that shall appear repulsive, yet the commandment to drink thereof shall not be repudiated. The Lord said, "Come to the place where I can give you bread and meat that you know nothing of."

Radical Voices

I beheld people in many places and lands hungering and thirsting for the bread and water of the Word. "These will be the days," saith the Lord, "that you will see men carrying the bread of life that will feed the nations of the world. I will raise up new voices that will sound the alarm of truth and justice, and you shall see My Face in degrees that you have never witnessed. This hour will be known as, The Hour of Radical Voices. You will hear radical voices on every front; political, world, national and international voices will cause such a stir that many will wonder if they will overthrow present day systems.

The 21st century will bring the glory of the Lord to a new height in the earth. I will take the worship in the House of the Lord and make the world system envious of what shall be produced. This will be the season that you will see the supernatural at a level that will be phenomenal."

"Beware," saith the Lord, "for there will be false anointings that will try to arise simultaneously. I will cause your eyes to be opened for the purpose of discernment. You will see individuals trying to raise up churches outside of the Body of Christ. You will hear or false religious that will come in the name of another messiah. This will be the hour that you will see masses of people deceived as they attempt to ascend into the heavens outside of the Door, Jesus."

Then the Lord took me into the heavens and said, "Listen." I began to be silent, and I heard the sounds of clapping in the heavenlies. Then the Word of the Lord came unto me saying, "Prepare for the downpour of My judgments upon men. While many thought there was just a sound of thunder, those that had an ear to hear heard the Voice of the Lord trumpeting commands to the warring angels and angels of judgment."

These will be the days that I will raise up prophets that will trumpet the word of change for their region and geographical area. I will bring forth a day of new prominence for those that have been placed into hiding. This will be the season and the hour that I will cause My glory to be seen upon these voices within a cloud that has yet to appear."

Governmental Corruption

I heard the Voice of the Lord saying, "Come up to the mountain of the Lord, and I will bring you to an unimaginable plateau of peace that the natural mind will need in this hour." As I silently waited in His Presence, I found a place in God that gave me peace of mind and brought calm to my spirit. The Lord began to say, "This will be the hour that this peace will be needed because of the vast injustices that will come forth in this hour. You will see a rise in corruption on every level. I will expose the sinister level of corruption that permeates high level governmental officials. Their dirty laundry will be hung out in this hour for all to see, and their shame shall become a proverb in the land. I will cause an upset because of the vital people whose lives will be lost as their sense of ethics shall sweep out of control.

Hunger for Prophetic Ministry

"The Word of the Lord will have a very special place within the earth, for I shall touch the palates of men, and give them an appetite for prophetic ministry. Men and women shall literally cry out to receive a fresh word from the mouth of God. I will cause men that were in a state of famine to hunger and thirst for My Essence to be spoken into their lives, and they will begin to run after those that have the Word of the Lord upon their lips. It will be the season that I will bring stability to the bases of those that will represent My Name," saith the Lord.

The earth began to quake under my feet, signaling the appearance of four angels with golden trumpets in their hands. I was perplexed as I noticed that they were riding upon horses that were prepared for war. Then the Word of the Lord came unto me saying. "This is the hour that I will cause a destroying angel to sweep across the continents of the earth and judge men who have refused to know My Name and My ways by way of diseases that shall relentlessly devour their flesh." The angels began to blow their trumpets heralding the day of the mournful lamentations of men. I began to hold my ears, for I could not face the torment of men's souls and listen to the hideous sounds of weeping and despair. I beseeched the Lord for mercy, and waited as the sounds of anguish began to wane. Then the Word of the Lord came forth out of the trumpets in a song of jubilation saying, "It is time for men to repent of their words and deeds… come and worship the Lord in the beauty of holiness!"

I fell down upon my knees and began to worship the Lord and the Lamb that was sitting upon the Throne. He commanded me to stand upon my feet, and announce that the hour has now come for the prophets in the earth to arise upon their feet and go forth as a mighty army and trumpet the Word of the Lord for their generation.

I prophesied as I was commanded. Then the clouds began to gather as this army began to wield the swords within their mouths and split men asunder from their heads down to their feet, like the curtains of the Temple that were rent from the top down. I stood in amazement as I saw this army coming forth in such power and authority to destroy the philosophies of men that have exalted themselves against the thoughts of God. The hand of the Lord shall slay leaders upon the earth that have swayed the masses with a gospel that preached against the knowledge of God, and you will see a generation destroyed as if they never existed.

Then I heard a voice sounding from a distance that was coming closer and closer. Faces began to appear in the sky as if it were a choir suspended in the air. The Word of the Lord came unto me saying, "Look up! Listen to the new sound that has been declaring the beginning and the end of My purpose." The voices spanned from one generation to next, sounding within the range of infinity, and gave a proclamation stating that the purpose of man is to glorify God and that none other is to share in the praise that is due Him. Man must learn to humble himself and submit to the will of God.

The Presence of the Lord appeared upon the scene and I began to discern the presence of His throne and I saw a rod within His hand. I listened in awe as God gave commands unto angels and spoke unto men, assigning them to specific geographical locations to which they were called to speak on His behalf. Then the words of the Scripture came alive unto me, and I understood that the Lord inhabits the praises of His people. I saw the Cathedra of the Most High, judging the earth, as men were praising the Lord.

I began to witness creatures that I could not describe because I could not associate them with anything that I had seen within the earth realm. As I peered at them in amazement, the Lord said, "This will be the hour that I will cause great upset to come to the children of men. Run! Run! RUN! For you will witness the Hand of the Lord come swiftly to remove a generation that has refused to exalt My Name upon the earth."

West Coast and Pacific Ocean

"Now go quickly, and behold the Pacific Ocean." I ran towards the West Coast, and the waters began to rumble and howl, for the finger of the Lord created fear in its depths. The Lord came unto me saying,

"The days will come that I will bring waters unto the West Coast of the United States that will appear in the violence of typhoons, and many will wonder at the strange weather pattern that shall prophesy My disgust with the sin in the land.

But, prepare! Change your position in this hour and begin to laugh!" A spirit of joy arrived in the earth as the calamity of men increased. I found myself laughing hysterically in the face of afflictions, though inwardly my heart wept many bitter tears. God spoke yet again, "I am laughing through My anointed vessels concerning the visitation of judgment that men thought they would escape, but I am a Rewarder... even to those that refused to seek Me. The day of judgment has come upon them. This is the hour of breakthrough, for I have rearranged the plans of men, and none shall despise My wisdom for long."

13

Discipline the Children of Men

"These are the days that you will see the Hand of the Lord stretching forth over the land, as I bring forth discipline unto the children of men. For I will silence the mouths of serpents that are spitting their venom into the ears of the country, and you will see forces that have been appointed to dethrone the influence of the Church come to naught in this hour," saith the Lord.

"You will witness a downpour of laughter coming from the heavens that will disturb the principalities and powers assigned to that land. I will cause many to know Me in ways and dimensions that many have thought impossible. The day of great illumination is coming to the earth. You will see men and women raised up that shall operate by a different order than that with which you are familiar, and they shall carry a weighty word of the Lord for this generation."

Attack on Church by Government Agencies

"You are now crossing into times that your eyes have never seen. It will be the day that the House of the Lord will be under close scrutiny and subversive attack by government agencies. There are officials who sit in high places that have imagined to silence the voice of the Church, for they believe that they are God. They will exert a system of control in an effort to overtake My sanctuary and places of worship. But I will stir up My fury and bring calamities into the earth that shall bankrupt their established system of order. I shall confound them with a season of natural disasters."

Red Cross and Social Security

The hour is coming that the Red Cross will not operate as it has been known in the past, for they shall experience a time of great famine, and they will be in existence no more.

Men will lift their hands for help and find none, for I shall hide My face from those who despise My Name. I will slap penalties upon the Social Security system for their abuse of the oppressed, and I shall cause their monies to come to a standstill. The people of God must cry out unto Me for help, and I will set up treasures for those who know My Name. They shall know Me as their Shepherd, and they shall not want.

Prepare! The clock is ticking and the time of this season of mercy is running out! You will see swift movements in the air, for change is coming from all areas," saith the Lord. "It will be the season that you will see My Hand raised against nations that have allowed sin within their borders."

Puerto Rico and Miami

Suddenly, a great gust of wind enveloped me, and as I looked towards the East, I saw a horrendous wind blast great devastation upon the shores of the East Coast of America. "I shall express My fury before the turn of the century, for I shall cause the winds to prophesy My judgments against the intentions of men. The borders of this nation shall be shaken with the hardness of My Hand. And I reserve a special visitation for the ports of Puerto Rico and Miami. I will demonstrate My displeasure and leave men astonished," saith the Lord.

Corporate America

"There shall be unusual calamities within the sky. Men shall strategize amongst themselves, and devise plans of their own imaginations to attempt to build a threshold of security, and their measures will become tight and oppressive.

I will cause a shaking within corporate America. Businesses will function under a great handicap because of the days of the judgment I have decreed upon systems that have worked corruption."

Airport, Bus and Subway Security Measures

"I will cause security to become tense within airports, and you will see a profusion of delays and long lines. This predicament shall extend beyond airports, and I will show this same sign at major train and bus stations."

Bomb Squads

"Bomb squads shall increase in numbers and in usage. Men will watch in amazement, and wonder why these things are happening before their

eyes. *I despise the sin that flaunts itself before My eyes, sitting in high places while boasting of its vanity. The ungodly shall reach their appointed hour of turmoil, and men will seek to hide and find no hiding place.*"

Television Station Under Siege

America shall witness the time that a particular television station will be under siege. Many will mourn and soberly wonder how these things could happen within the walls of a nation that once was so stable.

Global American Hatred

The hatred of America will increase around the globe. And you will hear of men telling America to get out of their business and to exit their nation. America's garment of nobility shall be seen as the tattered rags of intrusion. The people of these lands shall reject America's overtures, and they shall screech, "Preside over your own destiny, and leave us to ourselves!"

American Troops

"*You shall see American troops in many more parts of the world, but the relationships will be very tense; there shall be wars in diverse places,*" saith the Lord.

Abortion and Mercy Killing

"The hour of wrath will also come to the abortion generation. Not only will killings multiply, but you shall see the institution of mercy killing.

Many shall think this will be aimed only at the elderly, but laws shall be passed that will target the handicapped and emotionally disturbed, and many shall be the bitter tears that shall be shed over this evil."

Earthquakes: Strange Places—Strange Times

"When this hour comes, "saith the Lord, "I will cause the earth to shake and quake with the nausea within My belly.

You will see and hear of earthquakes in strange places and at strange times.

A day will come when the earth will shake during a major event and will eradicate entire families in a single stroke. Your eyes will behold My dealings, and I shall turn a deaf ear to your intercessions, for the cry of vengeance from the blood of the innocent shall dry out your pleas for mercy. People that know My Name must cover themselves in prayer, for they shall discover the power of My blood. It will be as it was in the days of Egypt, when the children of Israel had to place the blood upon the doorpost so that the death angel would pass over them. My people will experience this reality," saith the Lord."

Merging Military Forces

"You will see the days when walls shall come crashing down as major empires collapse overnight. I will show you days of major upheavals within nations that appeared to be unshakable strongholds. You will see military defense forces increases in large numbers."

Dollar Loses Its Power

"The season of intense technology shall be upon the land. You will see military forces merging in an attempt to gather more strength. Nations that you never thought would come into power will enter into mutual agreements, and you will see My Hand separate the wheat and the tares.

> *"Prepare! The dollar will lose its power, and you will behold another currency taking root within the hands of Americans. And this change will be blamed upon the economic collapse of the monetary system.*

This change shall happen in a moment; in the twinkling of a greedy eye," saith the Lord." "Once those that manipulate the monetary system get their plan approved, you will see new money surface within the hands of the citizens of this nation. The day of privacy will be eliminated off the planet, and new technology will chart the movements of men and women. It will be the season of the unveiling of great secrets."

Change in Media

"Media will undergo a change and will not be known as you know it today. There shall be great interaction with mass media. Men will stand in amazement before their television sets to behold a massive explosion that will take place in the heavenlies. The effects of this will be felt within the earth's atmosphere."

Sun Burns

"There is a summer that is forthcoming where men will be warned not to spend many hours in the sunlight. You will see the sun literally scorching the flesh of men."

These days will bring the church into a cycle of prayer that will cause people to return to My House. I will use My prophets to trumpet a call in the earth and sound the alarm of My judgments in these events. Prepare! For this day will bring clarity to this generation and unfold My purpose unto them for this season. I call for repentance, for the great work that is coming will not tolerate the deeds or thoughts of yesterday. They cannot enter this new season."

Strange Diseases

"I saw the judgment of the Lord coming into the earth. Strange diseases came upon the shores of America, and entire geographical areas were faced with great concern."

Entertainment Industry

I looked again and the Spirit of the Lord showed me a parade of those who basked within the accolades of men. And the Voice of the Lord uttered, "I cast a fresh judgment upon the entertainment industry. You will see the idols of the world fall overnight. I will judge the promiscuity that has reigned in this century to the defilement of many. I will bring the glamour of the entertainment industry to nothing, and you will hear a cry for morality escape from the lips of them that will apprehend My Name.

"You shall see great artists brought to nothing in their careers. You will witness the collapse of music that creates immorality. A generation will come forth that will boycott certain artists, and their actions shall demolish entire labels in a day."

Television Becomes Education Tool

"Television will be change, for this shall be a season of high technology. I bring great expansion in the areas of communication. I will change the way of education in this nation, and the media will become the educational tool of that day."

Racial Tensions

"I will bring about an anointing that will bring men into focus, and a new level of light will come to then nation at large. The days of racial tension shall increase, and you will see the ugliness of this sin magnified more and more. In the midst of the struggle, a major voice will be eliminated in a day. It will be known as 'the season of chaos.' My Hand shall be quite visible, yet My doings shall appear strange to thine eyes. The oppressed people of that day will cry and lament because a hero will be taken off the scene."

Hate Groups Vocalize

"You will see major religious leaders' voices coming to the forefront. It will be the hour of transformation. Clandestine hate groups shall emerge from their hiding places, and I will strip off their masks and expose their hostility."

Curfews and Weather Patterns

"I would cause the nation that has a pot on a fire to explode. Weather patterns will take unseasonable courses. My visitation will become great within the earth. It will be seen within the nation as curfews are established within major cities."

Erratic Economic Movements

"The economy will take a great change. It shall flip and flop with such erratic movements that men will not be able to chart what will happen next. Corporations that stand in the year 2000 will not be allowed to cross into the year 2001."

New Education Process

"I will bring judgment upon learning institutions that have enslaved the minds of men, and you shall see a new educational process emerge in this season and hour," saith the Lord.

Religious Wars

I looked up in the sky and beheld creatures flying as buzzards, looking to pick at the establishments of great strength. And the Lord said, "These are the creatures that have been sent to weaken empires and wipe out the names of those who have had coffers of wealth sitting in properties and institutions. This is the season that new billionaires will be made. I will bring forth a large segment of the earth that will come into great prominence." I looked up and saw Arab nations coming to the forefront. I also saw these as days of great religions wars.

The Name of the Lord will be heard by the people of God. It will be a generation of change that will begin to react from the defeat that has become a melting pot within the system. The day of great sorrow and collapse will come from hell to strangle the evil that sits in high places within the earth.

Youth Speak Out in Masses

The day of the Lord will bring joy to the people of God that follow His will, but great judgment shall fall upon those that have not followed the plan of God for this season. I looked across the country and I saw a mass exodus from many school campuses. I stared in amazement as a generation of youth started voicing their opinions concerning the ills of national and international issues.

I watched as the Lord began to hand-pick the next guard that would stand as watchmen over the doors of the cities. I saw men coming out of the East Coast that stood and proclaimed judgment against the corruption and injustices that had been established as law.

As I looked into the sky, an eagle soared out of the clouds and dived upon a prey which it quickly devoured. Then I saw the poor and the needy crying for help, and the Lord appeared to judge the deeds of the eagle. His Hand began to pluck the eagle's feathers. The nakedness of the eagle caused its senses to become dull, and the Lord began to speak, "The stripping of America is at hand, and I shall bring her to her knees. A stranger shall possess her financial borders, and I bring new nations to the forefront. Prepare for the great harvest."

Slanted-Eyed People

The Lord further said, "You will witness the slanted-eyed people coming forth from a place of relative obscurity. A new group of worshippers shall emerge from the East. Great orators will bring forth a clear word and a redemptive word to an oppressed people. They will teach the world about prayer and meditation. I will cause the nations of the earth to take a look at their value system."

I looked into the future and I also saw the education system falling into the hands of men and women from the east. The areas of discipline that began to be instilled within these systems of education began to fall apart. But the word of the Lord came unto me saying, "Men will reach for many things, but I am waiting for them to reach for My will and purpose in this hour. This day will be great if they come unto My purpose and visit all that I have in store for them."

A New Currency

I was surrounded by a sound of laughter which sounded snide and mocked the faces of men. I looked and saw the currency laughing within the earth. There was a great scurrying, and the dollar began to fall... fall...fall... and the nations around the earth began laughing at those who were selling large sums of items to salvage their investments. Then the word of the Lord came unto me saying, "A new currency shall come into the picture that will bring tears unto nations and commerce will change before your eyes."

New Foreign Alliances

Then the Lord began to send instructions to the new generation of heralders. In the year 2015, trumpets large and small began to blast a sound all over the earth to which all men began to respond. Media began to pick up this sound, and they echoed it in the earth. And the Lord said, "I will bring thee to an hour of awakening. You will see the downtrodden rise up out of the murkiness of obscurity. The light of a new day will present itself, and you will witness the coming together of foreign nations which had refused alliances in the past sit down at negotiating tables and embrace their new loves. Mighty is the Lord of Hosts, and Mighty is His Name!"

Illinois

"Come away, My beloved, and witness all that I desire to show you. The day of the Lord is a day of revelation. I shall unveil My glory within regions of the country.

> *I will bring a shaking in Illinois, and you will see revival coming out of desolate places that will radiate towards the east and the west simultaneously.*

I have heard the cry of a desperate people and I answer so as by fire."

Out of the bowels of the earth I heard, "Hear My cry, and attend unto My words." Then the voice of the Lord came forth in the sound of a trumpet and said, "The time for your deliverers is now emerging. I will raise up voices to speak for those who have been rendered silent. These voices will speak with a political and spiritual theology."

Ecclesiastical Think Tank

"I shall gather prophetic voices that will take the church into a new level of worship and a new measure of prophecy. A new spiritual kingdom will emerge in the earth. You will hear of "think tanks." The hour is coming that you will see many ecclesiastical formations coming forth from the Spirit-filled church. I will raise up colleges of bishops. You will see orders of this day handed unto men that will impact and change entire geographical areas."

A Day of Great Mayhem

"I will cause a great period of revival that will come in the year of 2005. The drops will begin to fall. During this season, a bomb will be released that will shake the world and cause men to wonder in astonishment. The day will be called 'a day of great mayhem.'

The day of My Presence will bring about great enlargement to those that will not be afraid to proclaim My Name in this hour," saith the Lord. "I bring forth a new nest of eagles that will come forth in My House." I will cause men that desire to know My will to feed upon this manna while within this nest, for I Prepare them for the years of proclamation that will be set before them."

Legalized Abortion Comes to an End

"The day of legalized abortion, as you know it, will come to an end,

But you will see hate emerging within the streets after this period," saith the Lord. "Within the process of this change, I will cause the spirit of murder to become bound within the earth. Now you will see My handiwork calling men to announce the next commanders that will come to the forefront of the Lord's army."

Cost of Seafood Escalates

Then I looked and saw the tranquility of the sea begin to change into an angry, swirling mass. I realized that I was witnessing a great judgment at sea. And the Lord said, "The price of seafood will escalate because of My judgment. I will cause diseases to bring plagues upon the earth. You will visit a day in 1996 when new plagues will be introduced, and you will see the judgment of God. Men will try to keep it 'hush-hush,' but they will lie to you through the media. When you hear of the magnitude of these diseases, you will know that this is the beginning of the judgments written herein.

Now the days of clear images and pictures of the Kingdom shall bring men to new light. Salvation will come to many as they witness the great day of enlightenment. I will bring about an enrichment that will cause men to hear My voice, and the sound of Truth will become clearer and clearer. I will make men to know My hand in ways that will astound their minds. The Word of the Lord will bring men into a clearer destiny, and I will move men that have been stuck in the past into a brand new future."

Now is the time for the sons of God to cry out, "Holy is Your Name." Then went a mighty cry unto the Lord from the earth. The Lord will bring men into seeing the great vengeance of the Lord. And he said, "This is the day that men have waited for. I will bring an end to illegal institutions and governments that have been set up within the nation of America, for they will fall with a great noise, and there will be a great rejoicing within the streets."

14

Then the Word of The Lord came unto me saying, "This is the hour that I am about to move in the lives of men that have forsaken My ways and through their backsliding have compromised My standards. I will cause swift judgment to come to many people who shall meet with a sudden end."

Freedom From the Constitution

I was carried upon the wings of an eagle and looked down upon a map of the United States. My eyes beheld governments in turmoil. And the Voice of the Lord began to say, "This will be the day that you will see states forming ungodly alliances. They shall begin to demand freedom from the boundaries of the Constitution. Many shall say, 'How can these things be?' but it is the hour that the spirit of uprising and rebellion shall visit your land."

National Travel Permits

Then I began to travel the landscape and found myself detained at checkpoints. I was shocked when I was detained at the gate from one state to the next. I cried, "Lord, how could this happen in a country that was known for its freedom? How can these things happen in the land of the free and the home of the brave?" And the Lord spoke quite soberly and said, "This will be the hour that you will witness the institution of travel permits that will grant individuals license to travel from one state to the next. Many shall be perplexed, yet this is a judgment that shall be rendered upon a nation built upon lies.

Much of what you will see will be masqueraded with the name of the church, but it will be a church that will not represent a spiritual kingdom," saith the Lord. "These will be the days of many wars and great uprisings. You will only begin to taste of this bitter root."

Retribution

I heard the cackling of derisive laughter that pierced my ears, for it seemed so out of place as I grieved over the judgment of God. Then the Word of the Lord came unto me saying, "This will be the hour of laughter in the heavenlies. The angels of the Lord understand that the hour and travail of America's repentance has come upon her. The deeds of generations past shall make their visitation, and they shall show no mercy unless a praying people stand in the gap to temper the move of God in this season. America has a date with retribution, and none shall stop their meeting."

Greater than the Bubonic Plague

And then I heard the voice of Wisdom cry out, "Prepare! Prepare! Prepare!" And the earth began to open up and swallow an entire nation with a terrible calamity.

"This is the hour that plagues shall consume a vast number of people in Europe. These plagues shall overrun their boundaries and shall sweep the Earth with a terror and vengeance that shall be greater than the Bubonic plague," saith the Lord. "The hour is swiftly approaching that viruses will appear one after the other that will baffle and mock the efforts of the medical industry. I will cause those nations that have created diseases for the purpose of evil to taste of their own bitter medicine. Their judgment shall now visit the governments that have funded the creation of this nightmare, and they will taste the harvest upon their own shores," saith the Lord.

The original thirteen colonies of America arose and presented themselves at my feet. I asked the Lord "What is this I am beholding?" Then the Spirit of the Lord came upon me saying, "Allow Me to take you back to the days of the early eagle." I saw men that were moving in the mercy of God start to remove the idols of the land. But their greed caused them to begin to abuse and oppress the innocent of the land. And the Lord continued, "Prepare, for the tables are now turning and you will see the Hand of the Lord moving on the behalf of those who were cheated out of their rightful inheritance."

Financial Restoration

"This will be a time that you will see My visitation upon despised people. I shall move upon people about whom the world had said would have no hope. A degree of prosperity shall visit them that will overwhelm the masses who sat in judgment of them. Their envy shall cause them to say, 'How could this come to these who, in our eyes, do not deserve these benefits?' Many shall be left speechless at the miraculous moving of My Hand, for I shall work miracles in the midst of this people. I shall cause the oppressed to witness My plan of restoration in this hour," saith the Lord.

The hand of the Lord came upon me and lifted me above the capital of the United States. I saw every work of evil taking place in a nation that had lost its direction. I beheld men wrestling and grabbing for power, yet neither had earned the right to grasp the gravel of authority. I stood transfixed by the struggle, and suddenly I heard a creature screaming in the sky saying, "The hour has come for the fall!" And I saw the great wounded eagle plummet down to the earth with violence.

A great company of birds gathered from the north, the south, the east and the west, and they began to pick upon the fallen eagle and devour her. It laid helpless upon the ground, forced to accept its tortuous demise. The Word of the Lord sounded forth saying, "The hour is upon you that a government of uniform will sit in the seat of power."

The Bear Defeats the Eagle

Then the bear came from the east strutting onto the scene, whose head was held aloft upon the wings of pride. The bear sat smugly singing, "We defeated the eagle! We knew that we would win! We tricked them into trusting us… we fought them from within!" But then I heard the Voice of the Lord declare that the eagle's defeat was the result of her undisciplined ways. She was defeated because her promiscuity and unjust treatment to the poor and the homeless weakened her defenses. Her hedge was destroyed.

I pondered at the gravity of these happenings when the Word of the Lord came unto me saying, "This will be the hour of breakthrough in the house of the Lord! You will see prophets of different orders emerge upon the scene. They will be a new tribe that will come into place, and the body of Christ will see miracles wrought at their hands. The miracles of this age will bring us into a degree of light that will astound the church, and the world will press into the House of the Lord to see the movings of My Hand."

Water Shortages

"It will be the hour that blind eyes will pop open and deaf ears will be unstopped. These days will bring not only the healing of literal blindness and deafness, but you will see the spiritual condition of men begin to change," saith the Lord. "The hour of laughter will begin once again in the earth, but this time you will see My judgment swiftly follow.

Prepare, for water shall be cursed in certain areas, and bottled water will become a precious commodity. I will cause the price of water to escalate to an all time high when a series of events take place."

Terrorist Attacks

"You will see terrorist attacks occur within the nation that shall bring great loss of life within communities and cities at large. You will hear of water that will be poisoned and food that will be tampered with, and the creatures at sea will suffer great loss because terrorists shall strategize to release a noxious chemical into the ocean to destroy the life therein."

Miracles

"This will be the hour of change, change, and more change. You will see the manifestation of the Holy Spirit in ways that will leave you astonished. You will witness the Word of the Lord coming to pass before your eyes. The days will come that you will see the anointing of Elijah come upon men and women that will call fire from heaven, and you will see the miracle of the flames appear before your eyes," saith the Spirit of Grace.

15

Ohio

The Word of the Lord came unto me saying, "Prepare! For I will show you the judgment written for the state of Ohio." Then I looked up in the sky, and I beheld seven swords hurtling towards the earth. I saw twisters of every kind and great weeping coming to this state. And God said, "The day of judgment shall visit this state. They will see wrath in this hour."

I saw the eyes of the Lord roaming to and fro within the borders of this state, and the Lord said, "I am looking for men that will be willing to cry out against the injustices that have been birthed in this state. I am looking for those that will loudly proclaim the Word of the Lord against the sin of racism that exists within these areas."

Then I beheld a great shake-up and the Lord allowed a calamity to hit this area of America so that great attention would be brought to the nation concerning His judgment. I heard Him say, "This will be the hour of major changes within this state, and churches will be called to lift their voices and they shall come together out of desperation."

Floodings

"I will shake up the Midwest," saith the Lord. My eyes began to drift southward, and then I heard the Word of the Lord saying, "This is the time for you to behold a disaster as well as a miracle." I saw massive flooding that began to mount up and many declared "This is the flood of our time."

My vision was transposed, and I saw commerce changing quickly. I began to declare unto the Lord, "Why this sudden change?" And the Lord said, "This is the hour that I will cause water levels to rise to towering levels, and this will be known as 'the years of massive floodings.' I will cause the land to cleanse itself of all the debris and waste that has been contaminated by mankind." I looked down and I saw the Mississippi River, but its water began to flow backwards. As I wondered at this phenomenon, the Lord said, "I will show you how to recognize My hand in the land," saith the Lord.

"I will make the land repent for the unrighteousness that has remained within men. This will be the season that I will command repentance from men in high places, and you will witness My Hand as you see My words come to pass. I will cause men to cry out as they desperately search for the cure of the incurable diseases. This will be the time of the elevation of men that have truly known My Name. You will see new political movements emerge onto the scene."

Detroit, MI—New Political Party

I looked up and saw the Motor City. I heard the word of the Lord declare, "This will be the hour of many turnarounds and changes on every front. You will see strong political voices emerge out of Michigan, and the volume upon their voices shall frighten the masses. This will also be the hour that you will hear of a new political party that will emerge with great success at first. These voices will be received by grassroots people, and many shall attempt to follow after these liberators, but they will not be the voices that possess the true power to bring deliverance."

Now the hour has come for the hourglass to be turned upside down, and you will behold My glory in ways that you have never seen. I will cause a new breed to surface in this hour that shall speak with a voice of boldness. The season that will appear will be known as 'the season of God's judgment,' and you will see the earthquake and tremble at My approach. Men and women that appeared so stable will become weak in this hour. I will release a new breed of men and women that will bring the church into the 21st century."

Ohio—The Buckeye State

"The hour of My Hand will be seen. I beckon thee, Ohio, known as the Buckeye State. I will cause you to come to your knees in prayer and start running to men and women of God that have the answer for the season which you are in. I will cause you to see My doings on the 8th day of the month in a year that ends with the number 8, and you will see tears of weeping pouring from the eyes of many. Men will run for fear wondering if their families will come at all."

Climatic Changes

"These will be days that the earth will groan and travail with the cry for change. It will be the time that you will see changes occur within the climate. The natural disasters of the 20th century will begin to bring a change in the climate upon the earth. You will witness the rise of temperatures at levels that will break records, and there will be great danger lurking for those that sit in the sun. It will be the time when men will seek to do business as the sun goes down. The days of scarcity will come. I will judge the earth, and the creatures will begin to prophesy and echo the message that this is an hour of change," saith the Lord.

Wildlife as Plagues

I heard the rustling of wings above my head, and as I looked up, I saw birds of every species filling the air. I could understand their language, and they spoke unto the Master asking where they could lodge. Then the Lord began to speak saying, "This is the hour of major judgments. The houses of men shall be plagued by the intrusion of wildlife. You will see the days where the beasts of the field and the fowl of the air shall become an enemy and a plague unto men."

Trees and Fishes

"I will judge mankind for the destruction of trees. Trees will become quite precious in years to come. You will hear of new laws and bills passed in reference to the trees that remain upon the earth. I will cause creatures in the seas to change the zones of their habitations. You will see fish moving further up towards the north. There shall be major changes within industry such as you have never known. I will make My ways known unto those that will have a desire to follow My plan, for this will be the hour that I will unfold My purpose to the eyes of mankind," saith the Lord.

New Wave Music

"Get ready, for you will see a fresh wave roll throughout the music industry. I will cause companies of major wealth to be forced to merge with lesser groups for the purpose of survival," saith the Lord. "I will bring judgment through a new sound in the earth that will silence the voices of past recording artists. This will be known as New Wave music. You will hear of a crowd that will pick this up and change the entire drumbeat of a nation. I will cause men to move with this sound that will speed up the paces of men in the earth. This sound will usher in a new level of industry. The industry as you know it today will become obsolete within the next 5 years. It will become so obsolete that you will see a nation thrown into economic disaster, for the hands of men will be replaced by the technology of that day."

Children Born Wiser - Geniuses

"Education will take a swift turn. I will cause geniuses to come forth within this nation. You will see children born wiser, and the learning process within this nation will take a turn. Many will say the system is not working, but the Lord says, "It is not the system that is at fault, but you are witnessing the day of removal of men with old mindsets. I am moving them off the scene. The hour of transition is upon you," saith the Lord.

Cancer

"I will bring about a healing in the area of cancer. But in this hour, new diseases will come forth that will eradicate entire communities within days."

Louisiana

"I bring places like Louisiana to a standstill in a season known as 'the lonely hour.' It will be a time of great disgust and the let down of an entire nation."

Men of Wisdom

And the Spirit of the Lord commanded me saying, "Make known unto men the tablets that are sitting in the heavenlies." He showed me a scroll that was written for the earth. The Lord said, "This scroll lists the generation that will come forth in wisdom. They will become legends within their own minds, and they will proclaim that they themselves are God. And this they will pronounce that all their acts are mighty. I will bring their 'wisdom' to utter foolishness. You will see tragic mistakes made in the heavenly realms where men dwell. You will hear of major upset within the planets, but when this comes, I shall tell you more," saith the Lord.

Major Discoveries

"I will bring about major discoveries in the year 2005. It will be the season of the unveiling of major events that will happen in the hands of science. I will cause entire textbooks to be rewritten because of the discoveries that shall emerge in this season," saith the Lord. "You

will find that I will bring men to a place of awakening their consciousness to realize that there is a God that is moving in the heavens on the
behalf of men. I will make the year of 1996 a year of turnaround in
natural disasters."

Hail Storms

"Shortly," saith the Lord, "you will see the plan that I have laid. Men
shall not be able to alter My agenda, for I have called for change." I
looked up and saw rocks coming out of the sky. He said, "You will hear
of places that will experience great hail storms. You will see the worst
episodes of the century within your lifetime."

Herbal–Medical War

"The medical industry will embrace a season of great challenges. A war
shall erupt in the media between medical science and herbal science.
The laws will change on the books and medical science will seek to
control all the plant life that I have created upon the earth," saith the
Lord. "But I will have you to know that I have the trees for the healing
of the nations, and no man has the right to assume that control."

Africa and Europe

Then the Lord said, "Come up hither, My son, for I will cause you to
see further things that I have written for the earth to experience."
Then I was lifted to a place and went to a golden desk that held the
judgments of men that would bring adjustments to mankind. Then
the word of the Lord came unto me saying, "Open your eyes upon the
page that is written, 'Present Generation.' Then I saw a line written
that said 'Messengers will come forth in this season with speeches

that will cause shake-ups in major countries. The power of speech will sweep the media, and men will come to know the days when the pen shall become mightier than the sword.'

I saw documents signed and the Lord said, "Prepare for the polarization of nations that will come into focus for the 21st century. Watch America form new alliances. The days will approach that the nations in the Middle East will come to a united front. There will be a religious war that will erupt and bring a great shaking within Africa and Europe. You will see the day when men will be placed into prison for their religious beliefs, and many will die in the name of religion during this next season."

Then the Lord said, "Speak to the mountains that stand before you." I did as I was commanded, and the mountains started to shift and a great shaking began under my feet. And God said, "This will be the season of the fall of major nations that have been standing in the forefront. Get ready for the next level. I will bring about major adjustments to those who are determined to know My grace in this season. I will cause laughter to ring out of the heavenlies that shall laugh at the calamities of men that have stood against My cause."

Price of Wheat Escalates

"The price of wheat will escalate and shall be priced out of the reach of the common man. I will bring judgment upon the wheat industry because of the corrupt usage that has destroyed the lives of men. I will judge the very wine that has intoxicated the nations, for I now consider the very root of it," saith the Lord. "The days will come that you will see the hand of the Lord coming in a season of much repudiation. I will make men to know that I am God, and beside Me there is none other."

16

"Open up thine eyes," saith the Lord, "and behold the wonders of the day. You shall now enter into a realm of the Spirit whereby you will witness the day of phenomenal miracles coming forth within the Church. I shall cause a generation of people to rise up and work miracles in their day. You will behold the glory of the Lord, for I shall reveal Myself in the heavenlies. You have crossed over into a period of time that you will hear of things echoing throughout the atmosphere, and miraculous events shall occur that will cause the faces of men to be mesmerized.

I will bring men to a place of accountability concerning the maliciousness of their deeds. Judgment shall begin within the walls of My sanctuary. I will make a people that shall stand before Me in holiness. I will cause men that have stubbornly ignored the beckoning of My Spirit and have continued in unrighteousness to be pulled out of office immediately. I will not suffer them to stand and receive honor that they do not deserve. Your eyes will witness a visitation of wealth that shall grace My House. I shall favor leaders that have an ear to hear My Voice, and they shall gather the wealth of the wicked. They will glorify My Name, for they shall experience My goodness in the land of the living.

Major Denominations to Fold

"The pillars of strength within the Church Age of the 1990's will be shaken before the turn of the century. I will cause major denominations to fold within the next 10 years.

In the year 2005, you will see a new group emerge that will take the church into the next 100 years.

They shall impact society in an unusual way, and they shall be a force to be reckoned with. You will see leadership emerge from this group that will become heavily involved in the political process. The days will also come that you will see men of color take the forefront in the church. You would say in your heart, 'They were always in the forefront,' but this is the day that I will bring them to a new level of responsibility."

First African American President

"In this hour, the day of the Lord will be revealed in a greater measure than that which has been witnessed in centuries gone by. You will see in your day where

I shall take a man of color, an African American, and cause him to win the presidency of the United States. Do not rejoice in this, for he shall be but a puppet dancing on the strings of manipulation, and the African American community will suffer greatly at the hands of the nation.

You will behold the ugly sight of the corruption of power, and I will begin to show the Church, and those that desire to know, where real power lies, for it lies within Me. I will bring men to an awareness of the many changes that will come about. I will reveal the plans that I have laid for this hour, and you will behold My glory expressed in new dimensions."

Immigrant Rights Revoked

"Many opportunities shall evolve, and a foreign nation will be enslaved within these borders. The doors of immigration will open again, but this time it will cause such a stir and a fury that many will literally come into the nation stripped of all their rights. You will see a system instituted that shall reek of the stench of slavery.

Many shall prosper in this season, but though this system will produce a spur in the economy, ultimately, it will cause a revolt in its future generations."

Strict Security Measure in America

An eagle began to soar above my head, and I stood in amazement as it began to perform acrobatic maneuvers in the sky. Suddenly, the eagle landed upon the earth, and the Word of the Lord came unto me saying, "The days of trouble are coming upon America shortly. It shall appear quite close to the home base. You will hear of the increase of terrorism, and security will be tightened within this nation. The security measures within this nation shall change in such a manner that it will defy your imagination. You will see the day that major department stores will utilize extreme measures of security and the streets will be filled with military forces. You shall witness the horror of calamity that shall strike fear within the hearts of men."

Subway Tunnel Shake-ups & Security Checkpoints

> "There will be major shake-ups within the tunnels and subways of America. You will hear of men running for the safety of rural areas, for there shall be great upheavals that shall strike great dread within the hearts of men.

You will witness a force in this season which you have never had to live with before," saith the Lord. "I will cause your understanding to unfold, and you will behold with open eyes the days when men will encounter security checkpoints just to travel from state to state. These days shall come, and nothing shall turn them."

Green Card

> "For America shall experience a season of great sadness. As I stood in the midst of a river of tears, I saw men walking with a green card in their hands. And the Lord continued to say, "You will see the day that the greed card shall license your travel.

These new security measures will even be used to determine who shall be educated and who will remain ignorant. I will cause men and women to ponder in amazement concerning the events of these days. You shall see the handwriting upon the wall, and mothers will weep for their children and cry out for vengeance. The days will come when you will hear of children caught in an explosion. Fathers and mothers will send their children off to school in great trepidation."

Cathedral in Commotion

"The days will come that you will stand in a place of humility. Churches will be called upon for help, for men will cry My Name in desperation, seeking refuge from their pain. Churches will be called upon for help. Yet those of evil intentions shall be blatant in their hatred of Me, and a major attack shall be launched upon a house of worship in the turn of the century."

> *I wept at these words and began to mourn. Suddenly, I heard a large commotion in the hall of a cathedral. I could not believe the atrocity that took place before my eyes. And the Lord said, "The eagle will be brought down to a place of humility.*

I will make known My ways, and you will see the unfolding of My plans. I will give an abundance of visions in this hour. And you will witness the function of the prophet in this season.

Prepare for great turnarounds, and you will see a supernatural element coming forth in society. That which was laughed at and ridiculed in the past shall become quite the acceptable lifeline for a future that danced with disaster."

Hate Groups

Then the Lord said, "Come and allow Me to show you the rottenness within the core of the nation. You will see hate groups within the nation that will become very vocal and they will trumpet their opinions of the government and despise the decisions being made. You will also witness organizations that will strategize a revolt against the present day systems and the way things are being run.

Citizenship

Simultaneously, you will also see men surrender their citizenship, and your eyes will witness a revolt within society whose noise shall echo for years to come. Men will be hauled off to prison because of their belief and conviction. The days will be upon you where men that do not bear the marks of this beast will not be able to buy nor sell, for they shall be expelled from a society that prays for their demise."

Farming and Fishing Industries

"I now show you the farm industry, for it will take a turn in the coming century.

> *I will bring a climactic change in this season, and you will see major rearrangement within the produce industry. The fishing industry shall also undergo major change."*

I saw the Hand of the Lord moving upon the sea. Then my eyes began to open wide as I witnessed sea life relocating to other parts of the sea. And the Lord said, "You will see the days of extreme changes within the climate. The days of unusually warm winters will become a reality. You shall see the temperature rising in degrees, even within the Northeast. When you behold this hour, know that I am rearranging things. I will cause industries to have to change strategies. I move in seasons, and will raise up one situation while I am yet taking down another," saith the Sovereign God.

African Nations

"You will see a rise in African nations, and you shall witness a day and a time that their influence shall bring stability and shape the affairs of men. I will show you that I take that which has no hope, and give it hope," saith the Lord.

The Dance of Nations

The vision of the Lord showed me a new room where the floors were newly polished and the room was dressed in beauty and glamour. I looked around and marveled at all the different countries that were assembled in the room of glamour. I saw ornate tables that reflected the distinction of each nation. I beheld them as they were in their native dress, and I listened as they spoke to one another in their mother tongue. Then the strains of music began to play, and all began to dance with glee. The atmosphere was full of joy for a moment, when discontentment entered the room. I noticed the year of 2015, and I began to wonder what took place before my eyes. The dance of joy became a dance of frustration, for the nations could no longer find fulfillment within themselves. They began to change dance partners, but their frustration continued. And God said, You have just attended The Dance of the Nations. You will see many new alliances in this season. They will align themselves for the convenience of the moment, and then they will switch to the next partner. But this will only bring a small degree of joy, for at the moment of their greatest pleasures I will bring swift destruction upon the thoughts and intents of opportunistic men. You will hear My laughter coming out of the heavenlies, and I will frustrate them further within their own frustration."

The Caribbean

"Mighty, O mighty will be the winds that will blow upon the shores of the Caribbean! I will cause teams to leave this nation to rebuild nations that will suffer a ten-year setback. I will bring men to repentance concerning their carnivals and activities that do not bring glory to My Name," saith the Lord. " I will raise up men that will call certain nations to repentance. I will make known My wisdom to those that will desire to hear what I have to declare unto them.

A new sound shall come into the earth because a new generation will make known the happenings of the Lord. You will behold the word of the Lord being declared, and great will be the number of women that shall prophesy in this hour. You will come to know My glory in a way that has never been experienced before. It will be the time that I shall unveil what I will be bringing men into on the other side. I will give the Church glimpses of My glory, and you will hear of miracles as young men see visions and old men dream dreams. I will make heaven known unto the earth in a degree of light that you have yet to experience. The Church will move from one level of illumination to the next," saith the Lord.

Comets and Eclipses

"The eyes of the earth shall behold a season of eclipses within the heavenlies. Unusual comets

shall appear in the skies and will be a sign and a wonder for all to behold. These will be the days of the dawning of a new age for fashions, a new age in science, a new age in industry, a new age in the Church, and shall impact every facet of society.

Technology will take off at the turn of the century and all the earth will prophesy and make room for new discoveries. You shall see this within your lifetime."

Church and Technology

"Even as I bring this forth, the Church shall be in the forefront of new technology that shall come forth in new levels. For I the Lord am raising up one in the year of 1995 that will take media to a new level for My glory. You will behold the day that men shall even capture My appearing in the sky. For as it has been declared in advance that every eye shall see me, technology will also make room and prepare for My coming," saith the Lord.

The days will come that I will judge those that will not change with the times that I am declaring, and you will find that those who choose to flow in a primitive anointing will be left out of what I am doing and stand ignorant of the way that I shall be moving. The days will come that you will see My anointing simultaneously captured upon the screen when I bring forth this major visitation."

Amazing Children's Discoveries

"I shall cause you to see a day that children will work miracles and come forth with amazing discoveries. It will be the Day of Amazement in the earth. Unbelievers shall come to witness the miracles. Many will never fully commit to Me, but they will see My Glory," saith the Lord." "I will cause men to see visions in images that will literally divide the Church as to whether it is I or not, for many will not comprehend My doings in this hour.

At the same time, you will also see that the prince of darkness will work wonders that shall be startling in their magnitude. Only those that have an ear to hear will discern that which is of Me and that which is not. I will cause you to know those that are mine by their testimony and confession of the Lord Jesus Christ. This will be the hour that men will ask individuals on national television, 'Who do you confess to?' in an attempt to discern whether they are of Me or not. You will enter a season where many prophets will emerge out of obscurity and stand in the forefront. Mighty deliverers will come out of Atlanta, Georgia; Washington, DC; and Detroit, MI. I will cause a merging of these three states because I will cause certain men of these areas to sound a trumpet in the 21st century that will make dry bones come alive. They shall stand together, and you will hear of major conventions coming forth that will liberate the souls of men."

New Political Party

A new political party will make its way to the platform. A candidate will come forth that will bring America to a place of trembling.

I saw devils in the heavenlies running amok with glee, asking, 'Is this the one that shall dethrone mankind?' There shall be a race that will seem to be very close, but the Lord says that this is the hour for shake up, yet it is not the hour for change. But I warn the Church: speak to the political arena, but do not allow yourselves to lose sight of your first love and miss the way. Remain on the course of a road, saith the Lord.

Carl

> "There shall be a man that will emerge as a voice to the nations. I was taken into the heavens to behold four letters, C-A-R-L. As I waited for greater clarity, the Lord said, "When you see this name appear in the media, know that major shake-ups shall strike the economy and foreign leaders will begin to lead this nation on a new course and shall bring you into a new destiny.

Many will flee the country in this season because they will despise the new alliances that will start to form. But beware," saith the Lord, "lest you become deceived, for fleeing in this season is not the job of the Church. I call you to anchor even more into your purpose to break the power of witchcraft that has dared to show itself within the walls of a country in a more visible way than anyone has ever witnessed."

A Great Home Going

> "Now come and see Proclamation of your Lord! There shall be a large home going in the year 2010." I saw eyes filled with water and America was shaken, for her eyes were plucked out in this season, and she mourned the loss of he who brought forth her vsion. And America wept, for now she was blind," saith the Lord.

The Season of Illumination

"Prepare! For I will make known the mysteries that this generation needs to hear. I will cause men to come forth with astounding revelations within this season. You will see the Word of God unveiled in a light so intense that many will stand amazed. It will be the Season of Illumination. The hour will come that you shall hear a trumpet sound in the earth declaring that the moment of change has come. When you hear this, prepare for the new guard that will surface. This will be the day that death will no longer stand as an enemy to man, for men were afraid to deal with its reality in the natural. I bring you into a season where men shall name their successors. This will be the hour that you will wonder how will this turn out, but men will come to a new understanding concerning purpose. You will see My Hand in a way that will amaze many and cause others to understand the time in which they are living."

Communities Quarantined

"Disease shall break out in many strange ways. A community shall come under quarantine, and the misery of pain and death shall walk their streets. I cringed as I heard their lament, "Oh, mountains! Oh, mountains! Come fall upon us! For our pain is too great; how shall we continue to live? Death! Oh, Death! Visit us now! Generations are dying and entire bloodlines are cut off." This shall be the requiem of a people who will sorrow, for they have forgotten about Me and are hopeless indeed."

17

ow come away," saith the Lord, "and allow Me to show you the major turnaround and the season of technology that shall bring about My coming in a glorious way in this hour." You will see the day that I shall reveal My glory in many parts of the earth. This will be the day of great changes in media. You will see the days of information increase at a frightening pace.

Men and women will be forced to re-educate themselves almost immediately. You will hear of men and women interacting through the vehicle of television, and you will see and hear men proclaiming that they are God."

Humanism Increases

"The days of humanism will increase and there shall be great controversy concerning the role of women within society. In these days, I will bring judgment upon those that overstep their boundaries. This will be the time of much turmoil," saith the Lord.

Alternative Lifestyles Confessed on Television

"I will cause a spirit of confession to sweep the land. You will hear of political officials standing before microphones, confessing their alternative lifestyles. I will display My glory in this season, and these days will be known as the season of 'media peeks.'

Mergers & Hostile Takeovers

"Then strange days came forth where the big fish showed up in the ponds and devoured the small fish. Even those that appeared to be large became small when these kinds of fish showed up on the scene. You will see the day not only of mergers, but your eyes shall witness hostile takeovers."

Cities Under Curfews

"Now come before Me, and I shall redefine the days which you have come through, and the days into which you are coming. I will make known these mysteries. You will discover major cities under curfews, and this will take place suddenly. The days are forthcoming that you will see and hear of the changes being made within big cities all across America. Come now and listen, for there is shouting within the heavens. The names of prominent men were called at the turn of 1998. These were voices that were discontent, but now they are called home to be in the Presence of the Lord."

Things Dropping Out of the Sky

"Come and behold more of the handiwork of your Lord! You shall see space technology make a major leap, and many that were in darkness concerning what men call 'outer space' shall come into a new light concerning these matters. You will also witness an hour where elements from that realm shall enter this atmosphere. You will hear of things dropping out of the sky."

Helmet Fortunes

I looked up and saw a season where men made fortune off of helmets. Men and women were walking the streets with helmets upon their heads. You will find men making astounding and frightening predictions concerning the damage that will happen when this massive object hits the earth.

I went to the television screen and saw America watching the take off of rockets and missiles on every channel. Many stood with tears in their eyes while others were waiting for the outcome. Then the word of the Lord came unto me saying, "This is the season that you will hear of things that will bring about many scary situations. Men's hearts will fail them because of this fear."

Meat Industry

"My hand will be seen in a greater dimension than has ever been witnessed before. This will be the time that meat industries will come under severe judgment.

The days will be upon a generation that will cause men to return to a diet of plants, for the day of meat consumption in the earth will be judged. You will see incurable diseases emerge out of diets that will cause viruses to sweep the earth."

Death in Sports Arena

"There will be three major deaths within the sports arena that will come one right after another. These events will astound the world. They will come fairly close to causing a nation to become spellbound, and many will wonder, 'what meanest this?'

The days will approach that you will see the mind of the Lord displayed in the form of miracles. Prepare! For these shall be the days that you will see limbs and body parts visibly restored in an instant. It is the hour that a generation will not only talk about the supernatural, but they will see it on display."

Black Out of Major City

I looked up in the sky and I saw all the lights go out. And the Voice of the Lord said, "There will be a blackout of a major city. It will bring great confusion to the streets and topple a city into ruins within a day. It will be a time of immense terror and from this even new laws will be put into motion that will bring great stress upon men. Many will suffer as a result of this judgment."

Days of Great Control

"You will also come into days that men will be picked up for standing in the streets or walking within their neighborhoods. These will be the days known as, 'the days of great control.'"

A.C.E.

Three letters appeared in the air above my head, A-C-E, and the Lord said, "When you see these letters come out of a government program, know that the time is near. Great shall be the sound of weeping and wailing, and many will contemplate ending their lives by suicide."

Stock Market Drops 500 Points

"The stock market will dip 500 points in one day and men will move about as if nothing happened. It will be a time where money, as you know it, will become worthless. A new currency will surface in the marketplace that will be a change in the standard of how money is weighed. This will be a season of unlimited resources that will come to the people of God. You will see new money coming not only in the streets, but it will also be the hour of new millionaires. Wealth shall come to the least likely to succeed. You will see young people come forth with large sums of wealth that will astound the mind of the average man.

What they will generate in the direction of technology will be unheard of. The age of these men and women will represent a day that the youth will lead the masses into a new tomorrow."

About the Author

Bishop E. Bernard Jordan is nothing less than a modern day prophet. In 1989 he predicted the 2005 Gulf Coast natural disaster, storm Katrina that had a devastating effect on the people in New Orleans. Sought after by nations of the world for his accurate prophecies, Jordan has prophesied the word of the Lord to literally millions of people. He is noted for his uncanny accuracy of the prophecies that he ministers. Businessmen, political officials, celebrities and churches are numbered among the thousands who have consulted Bishop Jordan for counsel and direction through the Word of the Lord.

The Master Prophet has traveled to Swaziland, South Africa, and delivered the Word of the Lord to the Queen and the Royal Family. He has prophesied in many nations, including Germany, Canada, Korea and the Caribbean, bringing an astute word of counsel to the leadership and royalty of those countries. In February 1988, he was invited to address a special assembly of ambassadors and diplomats at the United Nations concerning the oppressive racism in South Africa. He addressed the assembly again in February 1992, and prophesied of the impending liberation of South Africa, which has come to pass.

He has been featured on NBC's *Today Show*, FOX 5, *Good Day New York*, CNN, and many others. He was also featured in *The Daily News*, *New York Times*, *New York Post* and *Newsday* with some of his congregates as well as in an interview in *Billboard Magazine* on his views concerning social issues. His life-changing messages on reformation and liberation have sparked acclaim, as well as controversy, as he teaches the unadulterated Word of God. He is the founder of Zoë Ministries in New York City, a prophetic gathering with a vision to impact the globe with Christ's message of liberation.

Bishop Jordan has written more than 40 books including bestsellers, *Mentoring, Spiritual Protocol, What Every Woman Should Know About Men, The Power of Money,* and *Cosmic Economics,* and *New York Times* Bestseller, *The Laws of Thinking: 20 Secrets to Using The Divine Power of Your Mind To Manifest Prosperity.* He holds his Doctorate in Religious Studies and a Ph.D. in Religious Studies. He and his wife Pastor Debra have five children. You can watch him live on television on *The Power of Prophecy* telecast or through live streaming, just visit his site at www.bishopjordan.com.

FOR FURTHER READING

by Bishop E. Bernard Jordan:

The Business of Getting Rich: 12 Secrets to Unveiling The Spiritual Side of Wealth In You

Cosmic Economics: The Universal Keys To Wealth

Dreams & Visions: Letters from God and How To Read Them!

Prophetic Congress: Deep Calleth Unto Deep

Prophetic Congress: The Summit Volume II

Prophetic Genesis

School of the Prophets Volume I

School of the Prophets Volume II

Spiritual Protocol

Unveiling The Mysteries

The Laws of Thinking: 20 Secrets to Using the Divine Power of Your Mind to Manifest Prosperity

The Marital Union of Thought

The Science of Prophecy

From Pastor Debra A. Jordan:

Prophetic Reflections: Poetry From the Heart of the Prophetess

FREE
WRITTEN PROPHECY

As seen on TV !

To get your free personal written word
in the mail from me,
Master Prophet E. Bernard Jordan,
simply visit our site at
www.bishopjordan.com
and follow the prompts.

The Master Prophet will see the Mind of God on
your behalf and he will give you the
ANSWERS YOU HAVE BEEN SEEKING.

Index